Four Feet To Fame

A Hollywood Dog Trainer's Journey

by Bob Weatherwax

and Richard Lester

Published in the USA by:
BearManor Media
P O Box 71426
Albany, Georgia 31708
www.bearmanormedia.com

Printed in the United States of America

ISBN   978-1-62933-092-1 (paperback)

Researched/edited by Barbara Santorsa and Joseph Santorsa
Typesetting and layout by Darlene Swanson • www.van-garde.com
Photos from the Robert W. Weatherwax Archive
Cover design by Gary Lester

Dedications

For my sister Jo Ann
Although she didn't live to see this book,
she shared our unique childhood.

To Frank Inn and Sam Williamson
Besides having been great dog trainers,
they were my "second fathers."

For Tommy Rettig
Not only Lassie's first friend, but mine as well.

To Barbara and Joe Santorsa
Who made my fifteen-year quest for this book a reality.

Contents

Foreword

By Beverly Washburn

FOR ANIMAL LOVERS of any age, *Four Feet to Fame* is a must read. It's the never-before-told story of Rudd Weatherwax, written by his son, Bob.

For decades, the Weatherwax name has been associated with training many of the most lovable dogs in American pop culture. This personal memoir will take you behind the scenes, where you will discover what it was like to be a member of the most famous family of Hollywood dog trainers that ever lived. It will make you laugh and it will make you cry. You will discover both the triumphs and the personal sacrifices which were required to successfully train animals to act almost human in front of the cameras.

When I think back to 1956, my first year as a teenager, my thoughts inevitably end up on the set of the Walt Disney movie *Old Yeller*. Being an animal lover my whole life, it was my biggest wish as a child actor to be able to work with a dog.

It was my good fortune to be cast as Lisbeth, one of the three children in the movie, along with my dear friends Tommy Kirk and a much younger Kevin Corcoran. Little did we know back then that this film would become a major Disney classic. We also didn't know much about the man who trained the dogs who were to become our fellow actors, but we were soon to find out.

The Rudd Weatherwax Family: From left to right, Lassie, Jo Ann, Mae, Rudd, and Bob

Although it has been almost sixty years since then, my sweet memories of life on the set of *Old Yeller* are quite vivid. I recall the scene in which I bring a puppy to Travis, played by Tommy Kirk. The puppy was supposedly the offspring of my dog, with the help of Old Yeller, of course. The director wanted the cute little animal to be licking me as the cameras rolled. I had no idea how anyone could get a puppy to do that on cue.

Enter Frank Weatherwax. He told a makeup artist to apply some Gerber's chicken flavored baby food to my neck. The audience never spotted the baby food and the puppy started licking me right on cue.

I also recall walking into the makeup room one day to find the little puppy sitting in the chair. The makeup man was powdering him down with powder the exact color of Old Yeller. The puppy's coloring looked exactly the same as that of his movie dad. What a cute sight indeed!

It was Tommy Kirk who reminded me that Frank Weatherwax had a squeaky toy he would use to make Old Yeller look into the camera and appear to be listening intently. Unlike Lana Turner, who was discovered at Schwab's Drug Store, Old Yeller, whose real name was Spike, was discovered at an animal shelter. Not only did Frank Weatherwax make him one of the most beloved animals in movie history, but he no doubt saved Spike from being sentenced to death at the shelter.

Spike was destined to go on to animal stardom as the Weatherwax dog who brought Old Yeller to life on the silver screen. When I say that Spike portrayed Old Yeller all by himself, I mean just that. Most movie animals have doubles in case of emergency. Not so with Spike. In fact, it's safe to say that the entire production rested on this one amazing and intelligent animal. He performed all of the scenes by himself. Everything throughout the entire production depended on him and he came through with flying colors. He certainly deserved his claim to Hollywood immortality.

As child actors, we were required to have what was called a welfare worker on the movie set. They were employees of the Los Angeles Board of Education, and they were basically there to school us for three hours a day. They also looked out for our welfare while we were working on the set. As minors, we had to have regular breaks, no less than one hour for lunch, and we weren't allowed to work overtime or under dangerous conditions.

Old Yeller also had his own "welfare worker." That person was Frank Weatherwax. He took the greatest care of Spike, making sure that he always had water, food, treats, and plenty of rest in between scenes. In fact, I believe Spike even had his own dressing room and, if I recall correctly, it was bigger than mine.

Spike was a real champion, but I might be a little biased. After all, I actually got to work with him. I think Spike was a real method actor. He seemed to have a natural ability to interact with his human cast members and he took direction with the greatest of ease. Now, many years later, I realize that his personality and performance were the result of that Weatherwax magic.

There were so many innovative and clever training ideas used to create that movie dog; ideas and concepts that ultimately made the Weatherwax family true pioneers in training animals. How blessed I am to have been given the opportunity to perform with Old Yeller. I can proudly say that I worked in Hollywood with a Weatherwax dog. It doesn't get much better than that.

Introduction

MY NAME IS Bob Weatherwax. My father was Rudd Weatherwax, best known as the original owner and trainer of Lassie. My father and I were the trainers of some of Hollywood's most famous dogs. From my dad's work with Asta in the original *Thin Man* series, to my work with Einstein, the dog in *Back to the Future* (1985), we have created a long and storied legacy of trained dogs in the motion picture industry. Of course, the most memorable animal in our work was none other than Lassie, the cultural icon of both movies and television.

My family's journey began with my grandfather, Walter S. Weatherwax, who was a deputy United States Marshal in the New Mexico Territory. He was also an inventor as well as a trick rider in *Buffalo Bill's Wild West* show.

Economic hard times brought Walter to Hollywood when the film industry was in its infancy. At that time, some of Hollywood's silent legends were making their mark on American culture. Among the stars was a German shepherd named Rin Tin Tin. It was in that unique place and time that Walter and his sons, Rudd, Frank, and Jack, made their own mark on American movie history.

My father's brother, Jack, was the trainer of Toto in the classic *The Wizard of Oz* (1939). Dad's brother, Frank, trained Spike, the dog in Disney's *Old Yeller* (1957). Rudd, my dad, trained Asta, Daisy, and

Lassie, the collie who would rise to superstardom. I worked with Dad from the early 1960's until his death in 1985. Then, against my wishes, the Weatherwax family voted to sell the Lassie trademark in 2002. I continued to work with the new trademark owners until 2004.

This is a story of my father's genius and how he transformed the training of dogs from simple props on a movie set into actors who seemed to behave with humanlike emotions. Dad was a transitional figure in Hollywood animal training and my experiences with him from my childhood to his passing make up much of this narrative.

The backdrop is Hollywood from the silent film era to present, with a fascinating cast ranging from political figures to Hollywood's greatest stars. All of them came to know my father, myself, and Lassie.

This is not a sugarcoated Hollywood fairy tale. You will not find any worn-out Lassie stories. While the dogs are an important element of the Weatherwax journey, the true behind-the-scenes story goes far beyond that.

This is a story of my family and their common struggles in the very uncommon world of Hollywood. It is an unvarnished account of the toll Hollywood took on my father and our family. At times I hope you will find the story to be humorous as well as sad, heroic, and heartwarming. Sometimes this journey will take us to places where we must also deal with abuse, tragedy, and heartache. This particular Hollywood story has never been told.

In the end I hope that my father's lifelong labor of love will be uplifting in a world that, more than ever, needs some inspiration from the past.

Acknowledgments

THIS WEATHERWAX FAMILY memoir would not have been possible without the time, effort, and incredible talent invested in the project by several amazing people.

First, a heartfelt thanks to my longtime friends, Joe and Barb Santorsa. They have enriched my life in many ways, including their long-standing encouragement in many facets of my life, as well as a strong belief that this story needed to be told. Together, they have recorded and organized a mountain of interviews. They have edited the successful book proposal and every draft of the manuscript. They have negotiated with our publisher and continue to handle the business end involved in writing a book.

Secondly, I am grateful to have onboard the extremely talented father-son duo of Richard and Gary Lester. I first met these creative people when they came to my home to film *The Weatherwax Legacy*, an award-winning short documentary. I immediately recognized them as top-notch professionals in their field. As it so happened, we became long-term friends.

For more than a decade, I have tried to launch this book project. Unfortunately, every potential writer seemed to fall short of sharing my vision in print. Their style wasn't right, they didn't understand the big picture, or they wanted to do a tabloid expose. They had their sights set on something other than the lasting family memoir I had in mind.

When Richard stepped in as the writer, all this changed. Finally, we had the book I had envisioned all those years. Then Gary joined the team, supervising the visual content of the book as well as creating the cover image. They are truly amazing and this memoir is the proof.

My gratitude also extends to Beverly Washburn, who wrote the delightful Foreword and Ben Ohmart at BearManor Media, who immediately recognized the tremendous potential of this story.

Finally, there could be no story without the Weatherwax Family itself. Each member formed a part of the narrative's fabric. However, one person stood tall among all the rest: Rudd Weatherwax, who happened to be my father. This is really his story and I am indebted to him for it. We did not have a close, or even smooth, father-son relationship. Dog training brought us together and, at the same time, was a source of conflict. Nevertheless, Rudd Weatherwax is the heart and soul of this book and for that, I am truly grateful.

Bob Weatherwax

Prologue

Birth of a Memoir

JUST ANOTHER NIGHT at my favorite place. Nothing special, nothing different. The polished wood and glistening marble of the bar somehow always made me feel welcome, like going to an old friend's house. The owner was a friend of mine, maybe more of an acquaintance, someone you see often enough who mixes your drinks and brings you dinner. The combination restaurant and bar was only two blocks from my house so it was very convenient. It was much easier to go there than to plod around my own kitchen trying to figure out what to cook.

I was wrong when I said it was just another night. I knew it wasn't. Those that knew me well kept telling me that they didn't like the look on my face. They didn't like the look in my eye. Odd that I remember that but not much else in the way of conversation. Almost as a foretelling of things to come, I clearly recall listening to Jim Morrison's "The End." Over and over I heard, "Let me take you home."

I'm not sure if I was pale or appeared to be ill, but I sensed that my fellow patrons were looking into the depths of my soul that night. I stared at my drink as if it was a crystal ball, one that looks to the past, not the future. In that glass I saw my life, full of success, full of adventure, and lately, full of pain. I wondered how everything went so wrong. Surely some blame went to my choices in life, but many were beyond my control. I twirled the liquid in my glass as if somehow, when it settled, the answer would emerge as if from a witch's brew. The glass was silent.

My self-absorbed daydreaming slowly awakened to the sounds of the venue. "Bob, you don't look so good." A hand on my shoulder, someone quietly mumbled, "You don't seem yourself tonight." "Maybe I should take you home," another offered. Instead of accepting their concern, I shook them all off with the steely façade that came from a life of enduring hardship without complaint. "I'll be fine," I assured them, "but I think I'll be heading home." With my friend, Roger, at my side, I paid my bill and stepped outside.

The smell of the cool winter air and the bustle of traffic jerked me fully awake. Walking toward our motorcycles parked side by side on the street, I was reminded of a younger man who would stride to his machine with the confidence that he would always win the race. Back then, I was on top of the world and I never lost. As we mounted our rides, I felt a strange surge in my body, like maybe this could bring me back to the past of invincible conquest, away from a present of absolute loss. I put on my helmet and kick-started the engine. The motor roared to life and something in my gut roared with it. I thought, *Let's ride!* as we sped down the street and I could feel the breeze rushing past me, the air a mixture of exhaust fumes and asphalt. The road surface was smooth, nothing like the courses I mastered as a youth when I would punish my bike, as well as my body, as we twisted around corners, flew off the bumps, and swallowed dust like it was fine wine to savor. It was exhilarating. This was too, but in a different way. The smoothness of the surface allowed me to speed faster than on a dirt course in the desert. I twisted the throttle and the bike responded as if it was part of me. Faster, faster, the speed was like a drug. All my worries, all my regrets dissipated into the night air along with the exhaust from my engine. I hit the throttle again. The front of my bike jumped. I hit it again. The bike jumped again. I imagined the cheers from the crowd. They were rooting for me. Something I never experienced at home as a child.

The cheers grew louder as I made my bike jump again. Suddenly, I realized that they were not from an admiring crowd but from a panicked Roger. "Don't do it!" he screamed, as if he could read my mind. "Don't walk the bike, you're going to. . ." His voice trailed off as I threw away my last bit of caring and challenged death to defeat me. I hit the throttle again. This time the bike responded like a fighter jet nosing up for a takeoff. The front wheel rose in the air and I leaned back with one wheel left on the ground and my inhibitions left at the restaurant. The crowd cheered. The noise was deafening. Victory was just ahead, but that was not victory ahead. It was a line of parked cars and I was headed right for them. I was jolted away from my fantasy and suddenly realized this was not the desert. The reflexes of youth are not the reflexes of middle age, but muscle memory and sheer instinct helped me get the wheel down and the bike to swerve. It was too late. I avoided the certain death of a head-on collision, trading it instead for a painful reminder that I was no longer twenty years old in the desert.

As the bike swerved, the line of cars seemed to be moving in my direction. It really didn't matter if the cars were moving or I was. The collision was inevitable. Events seemed to slow, the Grim Reaper allowing you to relish the last moments of life as you desperately cling to them. I saw flashes of light, trees and cars upside down, then right side up. My body whiplashed from the now riderless bike and down to the pavement, perhaps my last resting place. All my senses were fading, yet I could still hear and feel my collarbone snapping in two and the sickening crunch of my sternum cracking open. The air was escaping from my lung as splinters of ribs punched holes in it until it finally collapsed, as I did. Then silence. The lights went out. It was dark, not nighttime dark, but the blackness of the absence of life. No pain, no worry, nothingness. I was dead.

"Forget the medical helicopter. It will take twenty-seven minutes to get here and this guy won't make it." I was not dead, at least not yet. My hearing was coming back and I realized that some time had passed during which a police officer had responded to my accident. The officer would have been right except there was one last person that night who wanted to help me. He was a stranger living in the building across the street and, to my good fortune, an ex-Army medic. He came out to see if he could help. His military training told him not to let me lose consciousness again. "Keep him awake," I heard him tell Roger, "no matter what it takes." Roger knew me well and he knew my triggers. He began to curse at me and slap my face. The rage grew in my body and suddenly all the pain of the crash was now transformed into the pain of my childhood. In my muddled mind I was a kid again, reacting as soon as I was touched. It was a rage that even death could not extinguish.

They kept me from completely slipping away. The medics from the helicopter had a live patient, although just barely. They wanted to cut off my jacket to work on me. Roger stopped them. The Weatherwax legacy, the story of my father's life, my life, embroidered on that jacket. At least save the jacket, if not me. "Take care of my dogs," my final words to Roger. With that, I was now okay with dying.

Then came the whoosh of the helicopter blades and I began to drift again. I died two or three times in their care. In those moments, I saw a rocky landscape that I didn't recognize. There was a man wearing a hat low over his brow. It was my grandfather, sitting on a chair with his gun and dog by his side. He died when I was two years old. I tried to look under the brim of his hat, but he lowered his head just enough that I could not meet his gaze. Each time I looked, the brim would drop lower, as if he instinctively knew that if our eyes met, I would stay with him forever.

I woke to the calming sound of oxygen surrounding me, gently blowing my hair. *Where am I?* Then I saw the strange hoses connecting me to machines I never wanted to be joined with. Panicked, pulling at everything in a frantic attempt to get free, I successfully removed what likely took hours to connect. The hospital staff rewarded me by putting me on suicide watch. My mind, still hazy, was drifting in and out of consciousness. All I wanted to do was sleep. *Am I dead yet?*

Many years and countless events have transpired since then, but I'm still here. For those who believe there's a reason for everything, that the Universe has some great plan for each of us, maybe there was a reason I survived. I'm not sure I believe that, but if you do, that's okay. Any way you look at it, I was able to stay here a little longer so I could tell you the story of my family.

My family has a unique history, especially my father. He gave the world something they will never forget. My relationship with Dad was complicated, to say the least. I loved him, hated him, and admired him. I worked with him, learned from him, and competed with him. Most of all, I am damn proud of him.

Walter Weatherwax

1

Walter Weatherwax, Deputy U.S. Marshal

NEW MEXICO TERRITORY, Friday Afternoon, February 28, 1908

Something didn't feel right. Apolinaria Gutierrez Garrett was experiencing a sense of dread from deep within her very being. Something was wrong, but she didn't know quite what it was. The stout, smiling stranger in front of her had rented a two-horse buggy and arrived at the ranch house to collect her husband. He was on his way to Las Cruces to sign a land deal that would provide the destitute family with some much needed cash. It seemed like a heaven-sent opportunity, yet Apolinaria's apprehension crowded all other thoughts out of her mind.

Apolinaria pulled her husband aside. Maybe he shouldn't go. Ignoring her fear, he headed out the door, climbed into the buggy, and rode down the rough dirt path leading to the gate and the road to Organ.

Within minutes, Apolinaria noticed that her husband had forgotten his topcoat. Even southern New Mexico could be quite chilly in February. She turned to her daughter, Pauline. "Quick! Saddle your horse. Your father has forgotten his topcoat."

Pauline raced out the door, saddled the family mare, and caught up with the buggy before it had cleared the front gate of the ranch. Her father expressed his appreciation by lifting her off her horse, holding his delighted daughter tightly in his arms, and promising to bring her back a treat from Las Cruces. "Take care of Mommy," he told her. Then he was gone. The family would never see him alive again.

Wayne Brazel, a young sheep rancher who was leasing part of the Garrett land, joined up with Pat Garrett and buggy driver Carl Adamson in Organ, New Mexico. Brazel also had a financial interest at stake in the land deal. When the buggy and mounted rider were approximately four miles from their destination, Adamson and Garrett both felt the call of nature. Adamson went first and then climbed back on the buggy. Then Garrett dismounted and walked to the side of the road to relieve himself.

The last sensation he would experience was a blinding flash of light as a bullet crashed into the back of his head. A second shot hit him as he lay on the ground, mortally wounded. Carl Adamson, the only witness, pointed to Wayne Brazel as the killer. Brazel turned himself in and admitted everything.

Approximately 120 miles northwest of the murder site, Deputy U.S. Marshal Walter S. Weatherwax heard about the crime. Not only was a fellow territorial lawman killed, but the very one who became nationally famous as the legendary man hunter who tracked down and killed Billy the Kid. Sheriff Pat Garrett, who lived by the gun, had died by the gun. Walter, no doubt, reflected on the fact that Billy the Kid had spent part of his childhood a few decades earlier right there in Silver City, New Mexico, where Walter lived. Most Americans viewed the murder as an open and shut case.

Deputy Marshal Walter Weatherwax knew better. He was well

aware that justice in the territories of the Wild West was elusive at best. Less than thirty years earlier in neighboring Arizona, another part-time U.S. Deputy Marshal named Wyatt Earp formed a vendetta posse to hunt down everyone connected with his brother's murder in Tombstone. Earp's justice came from the smoking barrel of his six-gun. He knew better than to trust a territorial jury in court.

When Wayne Brazel had his day in court for the murder of Pat Garrett, Walter Weatherwax wasn't holding his breath. Anything could happen, and sure enough, it did. Brazel looked the jury in the eyes and admitted unequivocally that he fired the two shots that killed Pat Garrett. He had no qualms about confessing that he shot Garrett from behind while the victim was helpless and indisposed. Garrett never saw it coming. Wayne Brazel, on the advice of his attorney, then claimed self-defense for shooting a man in the back.

What was even more unbelievable is that both judge and jury found self-defense very plausible. The jury, composed of all local Democrats, found Wayne Brazel not guilty. The killer of one of the territory's most prominent Republicans was set free.

In Silver City, Walter Weatherwax was not amused. Like Pat Garrett, Walter realized that financial stability for his ever-growing family was a more likely outcome if and when New Mexico became a state. Any incident suggesting to the politicians back East that New Mexico was still rooted in its wild frontier past could prevent, or at least seriously delay, those fervent hopes of statehood. The murder of a nationally known lawman and pulp magazine hero, followed by the ridiculous self-defense verdict which freed his killer, could only be viewed as a major political setback for New Mexicans.

When I was very young, my older sister would tell me stories about our family history.

She told me that our grandfather, who was born in 1867 in Kansas, ended up in the New Mexico Territory just like Pat Garrett, but for different reasons.

Walter was not married at the time and had an affair with a married woman, which resulted in a confrontation with her husband. According to the story my sister told, there was a gunfight and Walter killed the husband. His next thought was to flee the states to avoid federal jurisdiction.

Arriving in the New Mexico Territory, Walter used his natural talents with animals to train and ride horses for *Buffalo Bill's Wild West* show. Since the show traveled extensively and Walter had a ranch to maintain, he could not perform except when it was nearby. Folks back East had never experienced the Wild West firsthand, so Buffalo Bill Cody's extravaganza was quite a novelty. When the tour circuit included New Mexico or Arizona, Walter would saddle up and perform as a trick rider with the show.

In no time at all, Walter reinvented himself in New Mexico. He became a rancher, a family man, a horse trainer, a trick rider, and a part-time U.S. Deputy Marshal. My grandfather was also a Territorial Army scout. He was not a man who shied away from danger. When he worked for the Army, he would ride out into untamed areas to check for danger in the form of treacherous terrain or threatening situations. Perhaps Walter's most daunting challenges, which required great courage on his part, came when he helped deliver each of his seven children at home. Of course, one of them was my father, Rudd, who was five months old when Sheriff Pat Garrett was killed.

As a New Mexico lawman, Walter was only on call if there was a bank robbery or some other major crime where the local law officers needed him. He would then join the posse. Afterwards he would return to his primary occupation, which was ranching.

One day, as my grandfather was out working on the ranch, the local sheriff rode up from town with a posse. "Walter, get your gun and your badge. We're going out to arrest some bank robbers."

My grandfather saddled up and rode out with them. They eventually located the outlaws hiding in a shack. As the posse surrounded the small structure, a gunfight broke out. After a brief exchange of gunfire all of the outlaw brothers were dead except one. He happened to exit on the side of the shed covered by Deputy Walter Weatherwax. Walter could have shot him. Territorial justice allowed for lots of possibilities. He let the outlaw surrender, sparing his life.

As darkness fell upon the scene, the posse decided to spend the night in the shack. When the posse returned to town there were three dead outlaws tied across their horses. The fourth outlaw was riding upright in the saddle with his hands tied behind his back. He was the one my grandfather took alive. My father remembered asking Walter, "You mean you slept in the shack with those dead people?" He replied, "We were not worried about them, they were dead. We were more worried about them when they were alive."

Many years later, after my grandmother, Walter's widow, passed away, my father took me over to her house to clean out her possessions. There in her garage we found a letter from the surviving outlaw. It thanked Walter for sparing his life. He wrote that he served his time and went on to have a good life. For that, he owed a debt of gratitude to my grandfather. I was very young when the letter was discovered and, unfortunately, no one thought to save it.

2

The Flight to California

LIFE ON A New Mexico ranch could get lonely at times. Although stories of the Old West told of the lonesome American cowboy, Walter Weatherwax was not about to endure such a hardship. He soon married and began to raise a family.

My grandmother's maiden name was Anna Wallis. She bore Walter seven children and he delivered every single one of them at home. The five boys were named Judd, Frank, Mac, Rudd, and Jack. The girls were Dora and Peggy. Rudd was my father.

Walter was tough on the children, making sure they knew, without the shadow of a doubt, that life could be hard and unforgiving. The Weatherwax household was one in which everyone had to earn their keep. That applied to both humans and animals.

One summer day, a little dog followed my father home. You couldn't put much past old Walter. It didn't take long for him to discover Rudd's canine intruder. He told my father that he could not keep the dog. While he stubbornly stuck to his principles, Walter was not a mean or heartless man. Times were tough and food for a family of nine was hard to come by. Walter decided that Rudd could keep the dog if he was willing to share a portion of his own food with the dog. Walter also made it clear that the dog could not be in the house and must contribute to the family as soon as possible.

My father put a box outside as a makeshift doghouse for the little animal. At night, he would open a window and let the dog in to sleep with him. Then, in the morning, the dog would exit through the same window. In the Weatherwax home, no one was entitled to a free ride. At an early age my father found ways to earn his keep which, years later, brought him to the movie studio gates.

My father grew up knowing the value of putting food on the table. He told me that Grandpa Walter would send him and his brothers into town to get the produce that was being thrown away. They had to compete with other children who were trying to get that same produce. Food was scarce back then. They needed the fruit and vegetables to feed the animals. The other kids were there to get what they needed to feed themselves. The brothers had to fight the other kids to see who would eventually come home with the goods. I guess they were mean little guys back then. I asked my father, "Were you scared fighting those kids all the time?" He laughed, "Not as scared as if we returned home without the produce and had to face Walter."

As a highly talented and creative person, my dad didn't always use a conventional approach to acquiring groceries. It only seemed natural for him to make his beloved dog his accomplice. He trained him how to steal food. My father, conspiring with Uncle Frank, had a natural, instinctive talent when it came to training dogs for useful purposes. They bought a little rubber ball and painted it red to look like an apple.

Then they put the ball on a table between them and taught the dog to pick up the ball and bring it back. Fully trained, they brought the dog to town on his first food procurement mission. They let the little animal loose in the marketplace near an apple stand. The dog would pick an apple, run around the corner and bring it to Frank or my father. No one would run after a dog or even suspect that it was actually taught to steal apples. There wasn't a dog trainer in the world who could do that. The first Weatherwax trained dogs were taught how to pilfer and get away with it.

My father didn't just wake up one morning and suddenly know how to train dogs to do sophisticated tricks, like stealing apples. He began to acquire these skills back on the ranch in New Mexico.

Dad told me that while living in New Mexico, he would hide and watch his father work with his dog, King. Walter didn't like to train animals in front of anybody. He treasured the peace and quiet that could only be found in rural New Mexico, far away from any people. Dad and I were also like that. We never liked a lot of people observing or talking to us while we were training a dog.

Walter had a favorite place out of everyone's sight, away from the house. Dad would watch his father walk off and go around a hill to the place where he would train his dogs. Dad often followed him, sneaking up as close as possible, then lying down hidden from view where he would watch Walter work his magic.

Dad learned a lot watching his father from the hill. He thought Walter trained that way because he could do so with total, undisturbed concentration and no distractions. This way of thinking would become a major foundation for our future Weatherwax dog training methods. Human and animal needed to concentrate completely on the task at hand. Stories such as these of my father's childhood were rare. It was a hard life and his childhood was less than ideal.

My grandfather truly had a wealth of experiences all poured into one lifetime. He needed several part-time jobs to make ends meet. Perhaps his most important source of income was his ranch, populated by 450 Angora goats. Walter had a nearly all white collie named King who he trained to do some amazing things. One of King's tasks was to move the herd of goats in the direction he wanted them to go.

Walter would sit on his horse on top of a knoll where the dog could see him and where he could see all the Angora goats down below. Walter always wore a big white hat. If he needed the goats to move to the right he would take off that hat and wave it high over his head to the right. King would spot the signal and immediately begin moving the goats to the right. Walter just moved that hat back and forth and King would herd the goats for him.

At the end of the day, man and dog brought all the goats in for the night so that they wouldn't be eaten by predators. King was the very first collie trained by a Weatherwax. My grandfather could never have realized that, one day, collies would be forever linked to the Weatherwax name.

By the end of the first decade of the twentieth century, the Weatherwax family finances in New Mexico were running low. Walter started looking beyond the southwestern territories of New Mexico and Arizona. He felt the need to develop new economic opportunities. California beckoned. With a large family and little money, he must have wondered how he could even begin to realize his California dream.

While he distinguished himself in so many vastly different jobs, Walter Weatherwax was one thing above all else, resourceful. He knew that the sources of income he had cobbled together would not be enough to support his family. While he looked west to California for the future, he realized that he had to first do well financially in New Mexico to afford such a drastic move. Putting his creative brain to work, he concluded that planes, trains, and automobiles were here to stay. At a time when most of New Mexico's roads were still unpaved, Walter opened an automobile repair shop. Those horseless carriages were forever breaking down and there was no one to fix them. When Walter's auto repair shop opened, Silver City was able to boast that it had a shop that could repair those newfangled automobiles coming into town.

In between mechanical work, Walter spent his idle moments in the shop tinkering with things. In the process, he invented a new type of coupling for trains. He then sold the invention to the Northern Pacific Railroad. Suddenly, California didn't look like such an impossible dream after all.

In Dayton, Ohio, two brothers named Orville and Wilbur Wright, working out of their bicycle shop, were developing and perfecting a controlled flying machine that would allow man to venture into American airspace.

In Hammondsport, New York, another former bicycle shop owner was doing the very same thing. Glenn Curtiss started out as a Western Union bicycle messenger. With his brilliant mind, he was soon devising ways to deliver messages as quickly as possible. It was a natural progression for Glenn to go from racing bicycles to racing motorcycles.

In 1902, his ingenuity emerged when Glenn started manufacturing motorcycles with his own single cylinder engines. His unique carburetor was made out of a tomato soup can. Glenn soon attracted the attention of Alexander Graham Bell. Before long, Glenn Curtiss emerged as the Wright Brothers' chief rival in the aeronautical field, and is regarded as the founder of the American aircraft industry.

Walter Weatherwax was also busy inventing. Despite the fact that car repair shops were rare back then, especially in New Mexico, apparently so were cars. With a lot of time on his hands between customers, Walter worked on his inventions, one of which was the world's first high altitude carburetor.

At the time, Glenn Curtiss' aircraft company was involved in a bitter rivalry with the Wright Brothers. Curtiss could not afford for Wilbur and Orville to latch on to any new developments regarding motorized flight. The high altitude carburetor was a game changer for these airplane pioneers. Curtiss Company representatives wasted no time in getting together with Walter.

Negotiations appeared to break down when Walter insisted that his name be placed on the carburetor. The company was not willing to put any name on the invention other than Curtiss. My grandfather insisted that his name be included or no deal. They then offered him a percentage of sales in lieu of his name going on the carburetor. My grandmother always said that Walter was a real hardhead. He insisted that if his name didn't go on the product, the deal was off. Curtiss then offered a lump sum payment of ten thousand dollars, which probably amounted to much less than a percentage. Walter wanted nothing to do with the carburetor if his name was not on it, so he took the ten thousand. For the rest of his life he felt that Curtiss treated him unfairly, despite being offered a percentage. He couldn't get past the name. Nevertheless, that money was no small amount back in those days and it was enough to make the California dream come true.

Walter sold the ranch with his favorite knoll for very little. The goats and the auto repair shop in Silver City added to his cash, topped off with the ten thousand dollars from the sale of the carburetor to Glenn Curtiss. With his wife and seven children, Walter Weatherwax celebrated 1920 by buying a new home in Laurel Canyon, California. Now he could realistically hope for a better future for his family.

Little did Walter realize that California would become the land of milk and honey for several of his children as well. Like the automobile and the airplane, the motion picture industry was emerging from its infancy and becoming a visible part of the American scene. Coincidentally, it too had recently relocated to southern California. Walter Weatherwax took notice and soon found himself looking to the movie studios for a new source of income.

Rudd training Asta.

3

Asta, Daisy, and Toto

WALTER WEATHERWAX NEVER had a problem finding work and he excelled at everything he did. Despite his financial success as an inventor, he had to reinvent himself in California and soon found steady employment in a brand new industry.

Walter wasn't the only one looking to sunny California for a bright and successful future. While some of the earliest pioneers in the motion picture business opted to remain on the east coast, others, like the Selznick family, decided that the California climate was far more attractive. The movie people headed west, carrying their cameras and scripts with them. They found the climate in Southern California absolutely perfect. The brand new motion picture industry had come to stay. It was the birth of Hollywood.

Silent films became the rage. Although audiences were enthralled with Herman Brix as Tarzan, Westerns were the adventures they seemed to enjoy the most. Cowboy heroes like Tom Mix and Ken Maynard wore the white hats and sported the fancy six-guns.

The newly developing movie industry in Southern California was certainly good to the Weatherwax family. Walter eventually ended up doing extensive work as a trick rider in the films. As an uncredited extra, he performed much of the horseback riding for the cowboy stars. The motion picture income paid the Weatherwax bills and fed the family.

As children growing up in southern California, my father and his brother Frank soon found themselves following in Walter's footsteps. They, too, were trick riders at a time when Westerns were really popular. They started going to the studios each day, hoping the casting people would pick them for a role as an extra in the movie.

It was mainly my father and Frank who went to the studios each day. Because of the popularity of Westerns, Dad and Frank had more options for work as extras due to their horse riding abilities. Because of his riding skills and small stature, Dad was once cast as a stunt double for silent film star Mary Pickford. Mac and Jack didn't ride horses so they did not participate as often. The Weatherwax children were so poor that they had to share their socks. The rule was that the boys working that day got the socks from the boys who had nowhere to go. It was a simple rule, a rule of the poor, and they were certainly poor.

Being a clever teenager, my dad reasoned that his chances of getting hired would increase if he brought along a dog. He knew by instinct that a kid with a lovable dog had a real shot at getting picked for a job. Dad had the cutest little terrier, Wiggles, named after his body movement of choice. It seemed he never stood still. He wiggled. Dad loved that little dog but he also was sharp enough to discern that the dog could help produce income for the family. My father started training Wiggles to do a few tricks. Soon, both began to hang out around the studio gates and it wasn't long before the movie people took notice. My father found himself earning two dollars a day and a boxed lunch. He was in the movies and earning money.

My father was chosen for a scene in which he was to play a paperboy. He was supposed to give the newspaper to the dog and have the animal run and drop it on the lawn where some people were standing around talking. On cue, Dad gave his dog a signal and the little animal took off. He zoomed right past the actors and on into the house. When the scene was completed, the assistant director told Dad that his scene was done, but they needed the dog back the next day for an additional scene inside the house. That meant another two dollars and another boxed lunch. This was my dad's strategy all along, to get an extra day's work.

Henry East happened to be on the set that day. East was an animal supplier and trainer, but that day he was working props. In early filmmaking, the animal trainers were part of the props department where the various items that are used in the movies are kept. When Henry saw what my father did with the dog, he asked Dad if he was interested in training animals for a living. Dad said he'd love to and Henry East hired him on the spot. It was a career opportunity that would change his life forever.

In 1924, Dad was seventeen years old. Thanks to Henry East, he was on his way to becoming a professional Hollywood dog trainer. The strategy of using a dog to help him get work as an extra landed him an unexpected major opportunity in the big-time motion picture world. By the 1930's, Dad was getting some plum assignments. He trained dogs in such early classic films as *The Champ* (1931) starring Jackie Cooper, *Peck's Bad Boy* (1934), and *Call of the Wild* (1935). It was while working for Henry East that Dad trained Asta, his first dog destined to become a Hollywood icon. Asta was the adorable wire haired terrier in *The Thin Man* movie series. Starring William Powell and Myrna Loy, the films were extremely popular in the 1930s and into the early 1940s. Asta earned star billing in the opening credits, along with the main cast. This was highly unusual at the time.

After my dad quit working for Henry East, they remained friends. Rennie Renfro then hired Dad to train Daisy, the dog in the *Blondie* movie series. My father always brought along his brother, Frank, so that Frank could also have some work.

My father had many talents which enhanced his value in Hollywood. Daisy's puppies did not look alike but Dad was an expert with a stripping knife. He stripped down their hair and the result was amazing. The puppies all looked like Daisy's offspring.

Eventually, Dad and Frank left Rennie Renfro. Henry East and Renfro were basically just animal suppliers, not trainers. My father's philosophy was that if you're a supplier of animals for Hollywood then you should also be a trainer. The Weatherwax brothers were making a name for themselves in Hollywood as top-notch dog trainers and it was time to work for themselves rather than for someone else.

By 1939, there were three Weatherwax brothers who were finding their Hollywood fame and fortune training dogs. While my father and Uncle Frank were working together, my Uncle Jack was becoming a great trainer himself. His approach was a little different than my dad's. Jack would work a bit slower with dogs, while my father preferred to work more quickly.

Growing up as they did, opportunities for formal education were rare. Each of the brothers compensated for this in their own way. Jack had a talent for working with electricity and could have easily made a living as an electrician. My mother once told me that Jack wired my father's first house. He did all the wiring in Frank's house also. Mom said that Jack was better than a professional. With Jack's wiring, no one ever blew a fuse. He balanced the circuits with precision. Jack said that training dogs was like wiring a house. The analogy obviously worked since he certainly electrified audiences who turned out for *The Wizard of Oz* (1939). Toto was featured throughout the movie, appearing in most all the classic scenes in the iconic film.

Each of the three brothers made an indelible mark on Hollywood. They trained dogs who became the most loved animals around the world. For Jack, his icon was Toto. For Frank, it was Old Yeller. For Dad, Asta and Daisy were about to give way to the superstar canine of all time.

These men, who had little formal education, rose to great heights in the motion picture industry. That journey, filled with triumphs and failures for them all, would take on epic proportions before it was over.

4

Early Days in North Hollywood

RUDD WEATHERWAX DIDN'T have a birth certificate. He most likely came into the world in the family home near Silver City, New Mexico, on September 23, 1907. When he was born, New Mexico Territory didn't have birth certificates, at least not in remote areas. Families recorded important events, such as births, in the family Bible. Years later in California, Dad would have a hard time getting a passport.

Dad was never quite sure of the exact day he had been born because it may not have been recorded until four or five days later, or whenever they got around to it. The main thing was to get the child into the world alive, then go out and feed the goats, take care of the horses, and plan the evening supper. That's the way it was back then, in the really Wild West.

By 1927, the Weatherwax family was looking at New Mexico in the rear view mirror. Life was going to be much better in sunny southern California. The motion picture industry seemed to have plenty of work for transplanted Westerners who were skilled horseback riders. At twenty years old, Rudd Weatherwax also found time to get married.

My father's first wife was a woman named Emogene Barton. I know very little about her and much of what I do know was told to me by a longtime friend of the family, Josephine "Jo" Bondy. Jo Bondy, although born female, identified as male and was an African-American veteran of World War I. In 1928, Dad and Emogene had a son they named Jackie Dell Weatherwax. The marriage, however, suffered from the stresses of living with someone like my father and the fact that Emogene liked to party. Allegedly she had an affair and Dad, because of the transgression, threw her out of the house. Jackie remained in my father's custody. Whether they would have reunited will forever remain an open question since fate had other plans for Emogene.

Emogene and her girlfriends went to an amusement park one day and decided to ride the roller coaster. No one knows for sure why, but as the roller coaster winded its way around a turn, Emogene stood up. Whether she was doing it for the thrill or intended to end her life would be a matter of conflict in our family for years. On that day, Emogene was thrown from the car and fell to her death, leaving Rudd to raise their son, Jackie, alone.

Dad always blamed himself for her death, convinced that she committed suicide because he kicked her out. Jackie blamed him too, and this had a profound influence on the way Dad raised him. Jackie grew to be a deeply troubled adult. As my father rose to prominence in the dog training world, he had hoped that Jackie would be his successor. However, Jackie could not handle the pressure of Hollywood and the demands it made. This caused a great deal of conflict between my father and Jackie, and sometimes it got physical. I remember breaking up many fights. Jackie eventually joined the Marines, another choice that didn't end well. He was unable to complete his commitment there. Until the day of his death, Jackie blamed my father for his mother's death.

In 1931, when Jackie was a three-year-old toddler, Dad decided to marry again. This time it was to his brother Frank's former girlfriend. Mae Esther Hawksworth came from a well-educated family. Giving up her scholarship to Juilliard in order to marry a dog trainer husband did not thrill her parents in the least. As often happens, love trumped reason and her parents did not get their way. Their first child, Jo Ann, was born a year later in 1932.

Mae was my mother. She was very tough and very stubborn, traits she shared in common with the Weatherwax family. They were also traits she needed if she hoped to remain on a long-term basis with my dad.

Mom was an accomplished pianist which resulted in a scholarship offer from Juilliard. I found this out one day when I discovered some old paperwork indicating she had the opportunity to attend the prestigious school. Whenever I asked her about it she would never discuss it. I found out later the reason she gave up the scholarship. She was told by her teacher that she could not wear rings and could not play fun songs. When Liberace came to prominence with all his flash, she saw he was doing exactly what she was told a great pianist could not. She loved Liberace and knew he was an exceptional musician. When I asked her how she knew, she would just tell me to forget it. Having been proven right when it came to how and what to play on a piano was not enough. Not only did she never look back at Juilliard, but for the rest of her life she would never touch a piano. She was that stubborn.

My mother was not only very educated but also possessed a lot of business savvy. My parents once had an executive from Twentieth Century Fox over for dinner. Mom was a fabulous cook and he enjoyed two helpings of a great dinner followed by a piece of her mouth-watering pie. She then asked him, "Do we have the next job coming out of Fox with a dog?" My father said, "You can't ask him that!" The studio executive waved off Dad's objection, indicating everything was okay. Then, he asked for another piece of pie. My mother said, "Not before you tell us if we have the next job." He had no choice at that point. He knew what he had to do to get that second piece of pie. My mother operated with no holds barred.

The voice on the other end of the line sounded desperate. "We need a cat to sit on a mantle in a scene we're about to shoot," said the frantic producer. My mother quoted him a price. "That's too much for a cat," the producer objected. "For that price, I'll bring in my own cat!" "Well," my mother said, "the difference is, if your cat doesn't perform, you're in trouble. If my cat doesn't perform, you don't have to pay me."

The Weatherwax trained cat was hired. Mom was a shrewd negotiator. Indeed, the perfect business partner for my dad.

When Rudd and Mae were first married, Dad was working for Henry East. He and my mother lived in a very tiny house and there was no room or money for a kennel. My father had dog crates stashed in every corner. After all, working and training dogs was his livelihood. They were part of the family household.

Grandpa Hawksworth had been a jeweler and owned two jewelry stores. Grandmother Hawksworth taught English and had a PhD.

When Grandfather Hawksworth came to visit, he said, "My God, Mae, we raised you better than this!" Until the day he died, Grandpa Hawksworth was sure that his daughter had made a tremendous mistake and married well beneath her status. Although Grandma Hawksworth lived to see her son-in-law's success, my grandfather did not. Dad used to tell me that he wished old man Hawksworth had lived to see his achievements in the movie business.

Bob feeding the turkeys with his little helper, Freckles.

We had a lot of property when I was growing up in the 1940s, and my father kept every kind of animal you could imagine. We had a real menagerie including chickens, goats, and pigeons. By the age of ten, I knew how to milk cows and goats.

Dogs, however, ruled the roost. We had at least forty dogs at any one time. Of course, they had to be fed, whether there was work for them or not. The movie industry was very unpredictable. Sometimes long periods would go by during which there were no movies being made with dogs. We still had to feed our canine actors who were waiting to be cast in their next movie role.

Around 1939, my father formed a partnership with his brother, Frank. They opened a business called The Hollywood Studio Dog Training School. Over the years, a plethora of movie stars and prominent people were visitors to our home. The kennels on Van Owen Street in North Hollywood remain there to this day, where the original Lassie's footprints can still be seen.

Dad acquired most of his dogs for studio work from local pounds, while my mother kept the books, answered phone calls, and scheduled jobs. My father built the kennels on the Van Owen Street property. Those kennels cost more to build than the house in which we were living. They cost $14,500 in the early 1950s, when houses cost less. The Van Nuys dog pound tried to copy the layout of our kennels but they said that they didn't have the money to make theirs as good as my father's. They loved his design.

Dad really took great care of his dogs. Every day of his life, if he was in town and not on location, Dad would go out to the kennel to pet and touch each and every dog. After they retired, they continued to receive excellent treatment. All the Weatherwax dogs received superior medical care, the highest quality food, regular baths, and the finest kennels. They were better off than most people, having a permanent Hollywood retirement home, square meals, and the best of everything until the day they died.

We moved out of the property on Van Owen Street during the years Dad had a contract with MGM. Dad kept the small house on Van Owen although we were living elsewhere. Years later, after the Lassie contract with MGM ran out, we moved back to that house. Dad had to return to his core business of providing dogs to the studios. The house in North Hollywood had the kennels and a private phone line, a perk not available at our other place. When studios wanted a dog they did not want to wait around for a clear party line.

A majority of the dogs we used in motion pictures were adopted from shelters. Frank Weatherwax, my father's partner, found Spike in a shelter. Spike earned movie fame as Old Yeller. Frank Inn, my father's main assistant, continued this practice and found Higgins in a shelter. Higgins later became Frank's iconic Benji.

As a boy, I would often accompany Dad to the animal shelters in search of dogs with good movie prospects. Sometimes he would leave me home because I'd start crying when we couldn't take all the dogs home. Eventually, Dad just stopped taking me. He couldn't deal with all the emotions.

Rudd and Frank Weatherwax were successful business partners for a number of years. Jack Weatherwax, although not a partner, often trained and worked dogs for jobs contracted by his brothers. Their formal arrangement at The Hollywood Studio Dog Training School specified that they would each own and train their own dogs, but would split all the profits generated by the business equally. For example, Dad owned and trained all the Lassie dogs but Frank shared in all the money paid to Dad. Frank owned Old Yeller, but Dad shared in the money paid to Frank.

My father and Frank were consistent in the way they worked the partnership. No one owned the other's dog. No one worked the other's dog. At least, that was the way it was supposed to be. There were rare exceptions. For example, once Lassie was scheduled to be in the Tournament of Roses Parade but my father didn't want to do it. Instead, he sent Frank. I went along to keep an eye on things. Other than special events like that, however, it was a hard-and-fast rule.

Hollywood changed over the years as far as using animals was concerned. My father had chickens, pigs, and animals of all kinds. The reason for the menagerie was purely professional. Back in those days, when they made a Western, they used a lot of animals for what they called "atmosphere." A dog would chase the stagecoach coming into town, or cross the street while two people were talking. There would be a chicken or two walking up and down in the ranch yard when the hero returned home after a showdown. Since my father's dogs had to work with these other animals from time to time, Dad had them at home to get the dogs used to them. Also, for income tax purposes, they were deductible and we used the eggs for food. Dad always used everything on the property to feed the family. Nothing was wasted, just like on the ranch in New Mexico.

By the time I went into business, most producers stopped using live animals as atmosphere. Instead, you might hear a dog barking in the background but never see it. The soundman became responsible for creating the animal atmosphere. Animal trainers faced a new challenge in the 1970s. Latching on to enough big roles for their dogs, in order to pay the monthly bills, became harder and harder.

One of my jobs as a child was to maintain the kennels. Usually, I had the kennels cleaned around 8:30 or 9 a.m. One particular morning, I was behind schedule and hadn't started cleaning. Dad and Frank Inn came flying in the door.

"Did you clean the kennels yet?"

"No. I was just getting ready to."

"Well, we have to get the kennels cleaned."

We all went out to the kennels and began cleaning.

"What's the deal here?" I asked.

"Dore Schary is coming here. He's a big executive at MGM. He's right under Louis B. Mayer and he says he's bringing his dogs. I'm going to take care of his dogs for him," Dad replied.

Miraculously, the kennels were spotless in short order and just in the nick of time. Dore Schary arrived with his two dogs and was I ever surprised. He had two mixed breeds, not what I expected from a movie executive. They were from a shelter, had their nails painted, and were meticulously groomed. They enjoyed the very best of care.

It was obvious to me that he loved those little guys. Dore Schary liked the kennels and my father was happy that our visitor was able to inspect clean ones when he arrived. Just like boys, every studio executive needs a dog.

5

Beyond Rin Tin Tin

MY GRANDFATHER, WALTER Weatherwax, owned mostly working farm animals, but my father wanted to be in the movies. As a child, Dad loved to drop a coin in the old nickelodeons and watch images of a heroic dog named Rin Tin Tin jumping onto trains and doing all kinds of athletic stunts. He loved that dog because the animal was so spectacular. The German shepherd's courageous acts flickered through the machine as Dad dreamed that someday he could make a Rin Tin Tin movie. How to get there was the big question.

Lee Duncan's Rin Tin Tin was trained as a war dog. He was very physical. When Dad watched the interior scenes of the movies he noticed that Rin Tin Tin would just sit there with the people in the scene. The dog had no interaction with the human actors. My father saw this as a major shortcoming. He wanted a German shepherd star that would actually act and connect with the people, almost like another human. Dad thought, "What if I build more rapport between the dog and the people?" Instead of just having the dog sit there like a set decoration, he could be trained to nudge the boy, bark a warning, or wag his tail in excitement. With Rin Tin Tin, there seemed to be an inconsistency between the dog's action scenes and the dog's behavior in the interior scenes. He was daring and brave while jumping on trains, but merely an invisible prop in the family living room. Dad imagined his ideal star German shepherd as more lovable. In his mind's eye, he pictured the dog actually acting, responding to the human actors, showing emotion, and basically working the scene with the actors.

Young Rudd Weatherwax had his dreams, but it didn't seem likely that they would ever come true in Silver City, New Mexico. Then Walter Weatherwax moved the family to southern California and Dad's big dream began to take root.

In the early dog movies there was no sound. Silent movies had to have lots of action. Scenes with lengthy conversations were boring in the silent era. Everything had to be visual. With Rin Tin Tin, the audience thrilled to scenes of him jumping, running, and fighting. Lee Duncan trained that dog to do some amazing stunts, such as jumping off a trestle onto a moving train. Many years later, when Dad was a Hollywood trainer himself, he often said that Lee Duncan was the bravest man he ever saw with that dog, and also incredibly lucky. He never got Rin Tin Tin or himself killed or hurt despite taking all those chances.

When sound was added to movies, a whole new world of opportunity opened. Dad knew dogs could actually interact with the actors. In a way, the dogs were also actors but had four feet instead of two. Dad believed in the power of a dog's relationship with people. He always believed that every boy should have a dog, but he also believed that every dog should have a boy.

6

The Legend Begins

MY FATHER HAD a friend named Howard "Jack" Pack. During the early 1940s, times were still very hard and Jack was the kind of guy who would do anything honest, or otherwise, to make some money.

The owners of a collie approached him because he was known as a dog trainer of sorts. They wanted him to break their collie, named Pal, of the habit of chasing motorcycles. Jack failed. He simply could not keep Pal from doing this. Jack had no intention of losing potential earnings, so he hatched an alternate plan instead. He offered my dad half the fee if he could at least try to succeed with this dog. My father was busy enough with his own projects at the time and was not all that thrilled with the idea. However, Jack had done him some favors with German shepherds in the past and Dad considered him a friend.

Rudd Weatherwax met Pal for the first time. It was not exactly a match made in heaven. Pal had a mind of his own. He was fearless. Little did my dad know at the time that this dog's courage would one day pay off while performing in a dangerous movie scene. At that point in time, Pal was a distraction. Dad was about to realize his fondest boyhood dream. Although he found solid success in training small breed dogs for the *Thin Man* and *Blondie* movies, he always aspired to replace Rin Tin Tin as a canine movie star with a German shepherd who could actually display emotions on-screen. It just so happened that he now had the perfect dog named Kazan. It looked like Kazan would soon headline an action movie titled *Rip Goes to War*. Breaking Pal of his motorcycle obsession was not a priority. His motivation and interest level were low. Doing a favor for a friend was not quite in the same league as prepping his first German shepherd for a starring role in the movies. This was one of the extremely rare occasions where the dog triumphed over my father's best efforts. Dad did not break Pal from chasing motorcycles.

Jack Pack was not happy. He had visions of his twenty-dollar training fee going down the drain. Then things went from bad to worse. Pal's owners told Jack that they no longer wanted the dog. Furthermore, they would not pay a dime of the training fee. For Jack, the occasional animal trainer, it was a worst-case scenario, but he made one very smart move in the entire process. When he needed help with that dog, Jack Pack turned to my dad, and Rudd Weatherwax could be a very generous man when he wanted to be. When Jack informed my father that the owners would neither pay him nor take back the dog, Dad gave him ten dollars for the animal. This represented Jack's portion of the fee even though the owners hadn't paid. In an instant, Jack Pack had money and unloaded the unwanted animal. He had no complaints. Rudd Weatherwax was a great friend.

Now Dad, besides losing money, added to his kennels a dog with no apparent potential. Since he could not afford to keep a dog that wasn't bringing in any income, my father decided to take Pal to the pound. Pal was just another mouth to feed. There was no room for a mouth that wasn't helping to pay the bills.

My father was driving the dog to the pound when a wave of sadness came over him. He simply couldn't bring himself to do it. Taking a dog to the pound was against the principles he held higher than his financial ones. He saved dogs from the pound, not the other way around.

Dad had a friend who was a dog breeder with a sizeable amount of property. His name was Duke York. Duke took the dog in with the understanding that if Pal were ever needed for a movie job, Dad had the right to use him. They called that "farming the dog out" and it was a common practice in the motion picture industry.

My father had no intention of ever using him. Pal was an unwanted, unloved collie. Consigned to a farm, poor Pal couldn't even find any motorcycles to chase. This unwanted collie had only one stroke of good luck in his short life up to that point. After a last minute change of heart, Hollywood's most prominent dog trainer had a meltdown of the heart and decided to save him from sure death at the pound.

Pal, the original Lassie

7

Lassie Comes Home

ISADORE SCHARY SELDOM used his real first name. His colleagues knew him as Dore. When anyone at the studio met him for the first time, they were shocked to see a man standing before them. They assumed Dore was short for Dora and they fully expected to be meeting with a woman.

Dore was no ordinary man. Esther Williams once described him as rude, cruel, and imperious. Some would say that he was no different than MGM's top executive, Louis B. Mayer. Dore Schary was, without a doubt, one of the superstar writers who MGM had acquired during the Golden Age of Hollywood. His first really memorable screenplay warmed the hearts of movie audiences as they flocked to the theaters to see Spencer Tracy and Mickey Rooney perform in the classic film, *Boys Town* (1938). Dore scored again with the screenplay for *Young Tom Edison* (1940). His star was rising at MGM despite the fact that he and Louis B. Mayer had different philosophies regarding the types of movies the studio should be making. Perhaps because of this friction, in 1942 Isadore Schary was shuffled out of the studio's mainstream division and put in charge of the far less glamorous B-Unit.

In his two years in movie purgatory, Dore produced several films long forgotten by audiences, such as *Joe Smith, American* (1942) and *Kid Glove Killer* (1942). By 1943, he was getting better material. Projects like the successful war movie *Bataan* (1943) were attracting notice. By then the Great Depression was in the past and people were returning to the theaters for relaxation and entertainment. In fact, they flocked to the refrigerated air palaces, keeping the box offices busy year-round. The economy was at full employment, with people working overtime to keep pace with the war effort. Yet with so many commodities being rationed, they had fewer choices of where to spend the money. This situation proved to be a bonanza for Hollywood.

Dore's strategy was to follow up *Bataan* with another war movie, *Rip Goes to War*. The war movies seemed popular with the ever-growing audiences. *Rip Goes to War* would feature a German shepherd in the starring role. Dore knew just who to call for this project. Rudd Weatherwax was a successful Hollywood dog trainer who just happened to have a German shepherd named Kazan. Having secured his reputation as an expert animal trainer, Rudd realized his childhood dream when Dore Schary offered him the project. Dad started training Kazan, who he had no doubt would become the next Rin Tin Tin.

During this same time, Dore Schary was also in charge of a project titled *Lassie Come Home* (1943). He offered the directing job for the film to Fred Wilcox. Wilcox started his career at MGM at the age of twenty-two as an assistant director in *Hallelujah* (1929). He toiled for fourteen years at MGM and now he was offered a low budget black and white B-movie starring a couple of child actors and an unknown collie. Fred realized that this could be his big break and was determined not to screw it up.

Ironically, my father and my grandfather, Walter, competed against each other for the job of training and supplying the collie. Both were turned down. My father was just as pleased since he already had the job in *Rip Goes to War*. That was his chance to create the next German shepherd superstar.

Lassie Come Home was the story of a poor Yorkshire family who had to sell their beloved family pet because they couldn't afford to feed themselves, let alone a dog. The dog was sold to a wealthy man, then escaped and traveled far to come home to the boy who loved her. It was based on a book by Eric Knight and starred Roddy McDowall and a young actress named Elizabeth Taylor.

Lassie Come Home was a B-movie assignment, the kind of film that played in theaters as a warm-up for the A-movie. It was 1943, a time when theater audiences expected two movies, cartoons, a newsreel, and previews. Folks were turning out to movie theaters in big cities and small towns throughout the land. They were determined to reap the maximum Hollywood bang for their buck. As with most B-movies, *Lassie Come Home* was to be shot in black and white, not color.

The dog in Eric Knight's original story, *Lassie Come Home*, was a tri-color collie which is predominately black. The black color wouldn't show up well on film, especially in a black and white movie. Also, the camera would have difficulty detecting and defining the animal's eyes. Therefore, Fred Wilcox approved turning Knight's Lassie into a sable and white collie for filming purposes.

Wilcox knew that the box office appeal of his two child actors could not begin to compare with that of a Joan Crawford, Jimmy Stewart, or Jimmy Cagney. His future was riding on two kids and a dog. The penny-pinching unit production managers did not want to pay for a well-trained collie. Fred Wilcox, at the helm of his first major movie for MGM, had to make do with untested and less than ideal collies. He quickly found himself in trouble. The pure excitement of finally being able to direct his first MGM feature film, after fourteen years of going nowhere at the studio, was quickly evaporating. It didn't take long to discover that the MGM dogs just weren't working out. They wouldn't perform properly. In the indoor scenes, they just sat in the middle of the floor and stared at the handler, looking the wrong way while the family was doing the dishes. These were supposed to be easy shots and the dogs were ruining them. Fred was on the verge of tearing his thinning brown hair out. MGM would have had to cancel the movie if they had to cut out half the dog scenes in the editing room. The dogs simply didn't do anything. As a result, they were holding up production.

Wilcox began to suspect that the collies they had chosen were so bad that they most likely could not do the critical river scene coming up. Sure enough, trouble soon occurred on the set. A scene called for the show dog to jump into central California's San Joaquin River and swim across. It just didn't happen. Fred and his production manager sensed that the movie was in serious trouble. The unit production manager's job was to complete the movie within the budget. He was given a percentage bonus if he brought the movie in under budget.

Hiring the wrong dogs with no experienced motion picture trainer was costing a lot of money. The production manager not only faced the prospect of losing his under-budget commission, but also his job. If this film flopped because of the dogs, he knew he would never work for MGM again. Fred Wilcox also began to visualize his new directing career heading for the MGM cutting room floor. It was time to make a bold move and save the movie. The production manager reached out to Rudd Weatherwax.

When the phone rang, my father just happened to pick up the receiver. The *Lassie Come Home* production manager was on the other end of the line. "Rudd, you have to come up here and help me out with these collies. They just aren't working out. I need you to bring your collie here so we can shoot the scenes." My dad must have suppressed a chuckle. These were the same foolish people who thought they could use untrained dogs and make their movie without an expert trainer. They turned Dad down when he first applied for the job and now they were on the phone pleading. It sounded desperate. "I really can't," he answered, "I'm getting ready to shoot *Rip Goes to War*." That's when Dore Schary and his B-Unit people decided to play hardball. Before day's end, Dad was told that if he didn't do *Lassie Come Home*, he wouldn't be doing *Rip Goes to War* either. It was the MGM studio version of an offer he couldn't refuse.

My dad's next phone call was to Duke York. The collie that chased motorcycles just might be courageous enough to do a dangerous river scene. My father drove out to Duke York's farm and picked up a mangy, ungroomed Pal. Dad knew that he had very little time to get this collie trained and in good shape. In fact, there was only time enough to prepare Pal for just one scene, the challenging swim across the swift current of California's San Joaquin River. It was make-or-break for the production company and a feat the MGM dogs were refusing to do. Dad spent weeks down at the river where the scene would be shot. The dog was brave and willing, but he had to be trained by my father to do exactly what he wanted. Dad would worry about the other parts of the movie later.

Before Hollywood could bring Lassie back home, the daring collie had to survive a perilous river crossing. While he had been given a low budget B-movie assignment, director Fred Wilcox was pleased with the locations he could afford to use. Hugo Butler's screenplay was definitely not suited for filming on a studio backlot. The production manager secured an array of scenic places, eventually including some as far away as Seattle, Washington. It was very unusual for filmmakers to go out-of-state during the strict wartime gas rationing. Most of the shots were slated for nearby locations in California known for their natural beauty. They were places like Big Bear Lake, Big Bear Valley, the San Bernardino National Forest, and Big Sur.

The critical river scene would take place on central California's San Joaquin River. The river's headwaters are located in the San Bernardino National Forest. The natural background could not have been more gorgeous. Yet, staging an animal scene in the fast-flowing river waters could be every bit as dangerous as a German shepherd jumping off a trestle onto a moving train back in the nickelodeon days.

The moment of truth arrived. The fate of the Lassie production depended on the success of Dad's collie in the river. Despite the challenge the river posed for my father, he was definitely not a minimalist. He was determined to embellish the action.

Pal went into the water and the cameras rolled. Due to the strong current, the river was carrying the intrepid collie briskly along. My father was in a launch, out of camera frame, constantly calling and encouraging the dog. It all looked very dramatic. The crew was beginning to get excited. Finally, they had a collie that looked and acted believably.

When Pal came out of the water on the other side of the river, my father continued to add to the performance. He called it "milking the scene." Pal crawled slowly on the ground and then lay on his side, as if he were exhausted. Incredibly, it was all accomplished in one take. The crew was absolutely ecstatic. When Pal crawled out of the water, he was supposed to be too exhausted to shake off the water as a dog would naturally do. Instead, he collapsed on the shore. This was a very difficult effect to achieve and it required training by an expert who really knew his animals. It was a great example of Dad enhancing the dog's performance. Fred Wilcox was stunned. He turned to my father and said, "You know what? Pal swam into the water, but Lassie swam out."

Coincidentally, MGM was testing a color camera that the crew had positioned farther down the riverbank out of the way of the regular crew. As fate would have it, the color camera captured the entire scene of Pal struggling against the current. When Fred Wilcox went to Louis B. Mayer to tell him he wanted to hire this dog and Rudd Weatherwax as trainer, Mayer viewed the color film and sat back in his chair. He was stunned. "We're shooting this whole thing in color. Scrap everything we've done so far and re-shoot everything."

My father was enjoying a bit of good luck. The Lassie project was now looking more like an MGM A-Unit release. Although Dore Schary's B-Unit was still the production's official studio home, Samuel Marx was brought on board as the credited producer. Dore Schary was no longer credited.

In those days, directors would wait for ideal weather to film. Consequently, the *Lassie Come Home* production went on a brief hiatus before restarting the film from scratch for the color camera. This pause in the production allowed Dad the time he needed to get Pal ready for the movie. He only hoped none of the crew would ride a motorcycle onto the set. Pal would have found that very distracting.

The next order of business was to get Pal back from Duke York on a permanent basis. Dad recalled his previous difficulties with Henry East, Asta's owner, who kept threatening to stop him from using the dog in the *Thin Man* series. To avoid this kind of hassle, Dad and my mother brought Duke York to the house and proceeded to get him drunk.

Under the guise of reimbursing him for the food he provided while he housed Pal, my parents offered to pay him. My mother wrote him a check for $150. On the back, she annotated in small print, "Paid for Pal in full." She knew that if Duke cashed the check it would be considered a legal contract. Every day my mother would nervously check the mail for the cancelled check until it finally arrived and Pal was officially a Weatherwax property. The dog no one wanted had come home. After the movie became a surprising hit Mom was concerned that Duke York would come after Dad legally, but he never did.

My dad had a great natural gift when it came to working with animals. He instinctively knew how to teach a dog to convey its thinking when around humans, as well as in front of the camera. He literally turned the dogs into trained actors. My father studied actors including their timing and their methods. He controlled every nuance of a dog's movement, every twitch of the dog's ear, and every movement of the tail. It was all perfectly orchestrated.

He could also make it appear that the dog was doing everything on his own. That fooled a lot of people. The audience would see the dog pause for a certain number of beats, start looking back and forth as if thinking, then finally making the decision to jump that fence or cross that river. My dad was the man behind the magic. From words in a book, transformed to words in a Hollywood script, Rudd Weatherwax's skill brought Lassie to life on the screen.

My father liked working with Fred Wilcox but they did have their artistic disagreements from time to time. One in particular was noteworthy. During the movie, when Edmund Gwenn had to say goodbye to Lassie, Wilcox thought my father was screwing things up and he told Dad to disappear. Fred Wilcox, of all people, should have known better. He also fell into that trap of thinking the dog would perform with or without Rudd Weatherwax. It wasn't long before Dad heard them yelling, "Rudd, where are you? We need you on the set!" My father didn't return until the end of the day. It was an effective strategy and Wilcox never did make that same mistake again.

Wilcox eventually would direct three of the Lassie movies. He came to visit one day and everyone was having drinks in the back yard where my parents planned to put a patio. Our back yard had huge trees and Dad had a few cut down, leaving the stumps flattened off like little tables which became part of our lawn furniture. Wilcox had his drink on one of the stumps and, taking an ax, I started chopping on it. Each time I hit the stump his hand moved a little further. I guess I wanted some attention. Finally, my father got up and took the hatchet away from me before I chopped his fingers. I was only about six or seven. When my mother told the story she remarked that every time I took a swipe with the ax, Fred's hand moved another inch away. He was very nice about it and never made it an issue. He appeared to be a patient man, a quality my father obviously liked.

Throughout the filming of the movie, my father kept hoping that his dream job of working with a German shepherd would come up next. In the end, MGM cancelled *Rip Goes to War* and my father was part of the reason why. *Lassie Come Home* was on its way to becoming a huge success at the box office. Dad never got to use Kazan even though that's what he always wanted to do. MGM's super canine star was destined to be a collie, not a German shepherd.

My father had never given any serious thought to working with collies. They show emotion easily but that also makes them more difficult to work with on the set. They are suspicious by nature, as they were bred to be guard dogs and protect sheep. For that job they needed to be wary. Unfortunately, what they are bred to do is the exact opposite of what is needed in motion pictures. For the movies, the dogs needed to be outgoing, friendly, and not easily rattled.

Dad's first order of business was to have Pal spend time with each and every one of the actors. Once Pal developed a rapport with an actor, he could be more outgoing. When someone went to the sink to wash a dish, Pal followed along with him or her. When someone else went to another part of the room, Pal followed with his tail wagging. He was acting as if he was their family dog. There he was, at home with them in the kitchen, living room, or bedroom. It was all due to Dad's magic. Pal turned out to be true superstar material. His only vice, which he never gave up, was chasing motorcycles. For all his success, that one bad behavior was a small price to pay.

Dad told me to always be prepared. "Do the best job you can, no matter how small or insignificant it may seem. Someday you will be presented with an opportunity. It will come, and if you are prepared, you will be successful." That is exactly what happened with his German shepherd, Kazan. Dore Schary gave him his big opportunity with *Rip Goes to War*. Dad's lifelong dream of creating a star just like Rin Tin Tin was about to come true. Then Hollywood's capricious nature came into play and Dad ended up working on a collie movie instead. Rudd Weatherwax had his star dog alright, but that dog turned out to be a collie instead of a shepherd. At the time, no one could possibly have imagined the magnitude of the fame and fortune that was about to cascade down on MGM. No one suspected that *Lassie Come Home* was destined to be a mega-success at the box office as well as a classic film for all time. Lassie would become an American icon while *Rip Goes to War* was forgotten in the blinding glare of Lassie's success.

Frank Inn, one of the people to whom I dedicated this book, was my father's close friend and assistant trainer on *Lassie Come Home*. Frank Inn's birth name was Elias Franklin Freeman He came from Indiana and started out as a laborer at the studio, emptying trash cans, sweeping up, and performing general maintenance. He would work on different movie sets on the MGM studio lot depending on where he was assigned. My father noticed Frank always leaning on a shovel watching him work. After a while this got a bit unnerving and one day my father approached him. "Why do you watch me all day?" Frank told him he was an amateur dog trainer and would trade assignments with the other workers to be on the set where my father was working. He said he would love to get into the movie business training dogs, so my father hired him.

Frank Inn became another father to me. He taught me how to ride a bike and let me hang around with him. When I was a kid I could not pronounce the letter "S" so I would call him the "fart man" and he would correct me and say "That's the smart man." Since we lived in the middle of nowhere, I used to spend all day with Frank while he worked at our house with the dogs.

When my father hired him he was concerned about where Frank slept. He came from Indiana and he really didn't have any family or friends in California. Frank told my father that he had a job at a local circus taking care of the animals and he slept under the hyena cage. Dad once needed Frank to help him on a show and, knowing where he slept, was a little concerned about how Frank would dress. To Dad's surprise, Frank showed up dressed better than he was.

During the filming of *Lassie Come Home,* the crew traveled by train from one location to another. It was wartime and very strict gas rationing was in effect. Trains were the only option for a movie production company traveling all over the state and beyond.

While most of the crew enjoyed regular accommodations on the train, Pal was required to ride in the luggage car. Pal was not a superstar yet. He was just another dog making his first movie and hadn't yet made a dime for MGM. My dad and Frank Inn rode with Pal in the luggage car which was located at the end of the train near the caboose. They felt like second class citizens. The luggage car was not designed for passengers, so it was not very comfortable. Also, when the crew was enjoying meals in the dining car at the front of the train, they tended to forget about Rudd and Frank in the back. Occasionally, they would bring some sandwiches, but most of the time Rudd and Frank were out of sight and out of food.

Somewhere in their lonely car Frank Inn discovered a crate of apples that weren't quite ripe. His hunger got the best of him and he ate a few. It didn't take long for his stomach to revolt. Thankfully, the train had made a stop. Frank flew through the luggage car door to the caboose, jumped over the railing and onto the tracks. As Frank got relief, the train started to come to life and began slowly moving. Dad yelled at Frank who quickly pulled himself together and sprinted to the steps of the caboose. He felt much better even if he nearly lost his ride.

Eric Knight made the trek to Hollywood and visited the set where they were shooting the story first published in *The Saturday Evening Post*. He was fascinated as he watched my father work. The scene they were shooting that day called for Lassie to come slipping and sliding down a mountainside. Since collies are sure-footed, this did not come naturally to them. To achieve the effect, my father decided to change Lassie's gait by loosening up some rocks. As the dog came upon the loose rocks, he had no choice but to change his pattern. He began slipping and the effect was most dramatic. Knight was so impressed that he wrote a note on MGM stationery and handed it to Dad before he left the set. It read, "To Rudd Weatherwax, who knows more about collies than a Yorkshireman." This was the ultimate praise coming from the man who first told the story of the courageous dog. The words he scribbled on that note foretold an event that my father never could have imagined, that the dog that was about to launch him to the pinnacle of Hollywood fame would be a collie. Unfortunately, Eric Knight died in a plane crash before the movie was completed. Knight had a tri-colored collie named Tootsie on which he modeled the dog in his famous story. As a tribute to Knight, Edmund Gwenn's dog in the film was called Toots. He was played by Dad's dog, Shorty.

Arguably, Dad was the one person who saved the *Lassie Come Home* production when it was on the verge of total collapse. My father, for reasons he would never admit, worked very hard on this project, as if it had a greater destiny. I always believed that Dad had a spiritual sense that this collie, and this movie, was something very special.

The night *Lassie Come Home* premiered, my parents joined the audience to experience MGM's newest Technicolor movie. I, on the other hand, got to spend the night with a babysitter. At the end of the movie, people streamed out of the theater crying. Ushers said that the weeping actually started during the film and continued as the audience exited. My father was stunned and my mother turned and just looked at him. "I think we made a terrible movie," Dad said, disappointed that his absolute best work had left the audience in tears. It must have been horrible.

The next day dawned on a very disappointed Weatherwax home. We lived adjacent to two defense plants and the pillars holding up the camouflage protecting the facilities were on our property. One of the plants was a precision drill factory where they made instruments and various other items required for the war effort. Some of the plant workers saw my father in the yard. They knew him and what he did for a living. One yelled out, "Hey, Mr. Weatherwax, we just saw *Lassie Come Home* and you have it made. You hit the jackpot. It's a winner!" At that moment, my father began to think that the movie might actually be okay. The realization hit him that when the audience cries like that, it's a good thing. They loved Lassie and he was about to become the brightest star in the MGM firmament.

As is always the case in life, our wildest successes are often accompanied by the sting of sadness. My grandfather, Walter Weatherwax, who was still alive when filming of *Lassie Come Home* began, died before production ended in 1943. Walter had a collie of his own whose name was Boy and who was likely a descendant of his collie, King, in New Mexico. As anyone who has owned a collie will tell you, they are the most loving and loyal creatures. One look into their soulful eyes reveals a heart that is pure and uncomplicated, as it was with Boy. His loyalty was undying as he patiently slept next to Walter, who spent his elder years relaxing in his rocking chair. When a collie gives you its love, it is without conditions and it is forever. After Walter's death, Boy no longer wanted food or anything life had to offer. As the man in the rocking chair was gone, so was Boy's spirit. He remained next to the empty rocking chair hoping that Walter would soon return. After days of a lonely vigil, Boy realized that Walter would never be coming back. One night, he settled near the rocker one last time, quietly closed his eyes, and joined his master.

The circle of life was complete. The man who started it all in the wilds of New Mexico, moved his family to California, and recognized new opportunity in a fledging industry, was gone. He passed away just as his son, Rudd, was on the verge of unimaginable success. In the days when Walter moved his family to California and an uncertain future, he never could have foreseen that his decision would result in one of his sons becoming a Hollywood legend. It was all because of the unlikely events that brought Rudd together with a mangy, unloved collie named Pal.

8

MGM Loves Rudd

LOUIS B. MAYER was ecstatic that *Lassie Come Home* had turned into a box office success beyond his wildest imagination. Going to the movies was becoming America's biggest leisure time activity and Hollywood was as hot as the shooting war overseas. Mayer had always done the right thing for my dad. He agreed to Fred Wilcox's request to bring Dad in to train Lassie for MGM. He didn't blink an eye when he decided that *Lassie Come Home* would be filmed in very expensive Technicolor. Later on, he petitioned Howard Hughes to allow Lassie to fly as a passenger and not as cargo. Mayer had his share of critics, but my dad was not one of them.

One of the most important things Louis B. Mayer did for my father was to create a department in MGM in which Dad tested the temperament of dogs slated for overseas military duty. This afforded my father the opportunity to contribute to the war effort while remaining at MGM. The dogs were sent overseas, not to look for bombs, but to detect the enemy. They especially proved valuable in fighting in the Pacific theater. The GIs kept the dogs by their side to alert them to the presence of the enemy. Eventually, Japanese snipers started shooting the dogs. Dad heard about one soldier's dog who died in his arms.

The local draft board agreed with Mayer that Rudd Weatherwax was worth more to the war effort in his capacity at MGM. In addition, Louis B. Mayer planned for him to make a couple of good war movies featuring dogs. It was no accident that two of the Lassie movies featured war themes.

Although my father was never in the military during World War II, he did serve as an air raid warden. His job was to patrol the neighborhood at night, checking to make sure everyone's lights were out and their blinds were drawn. After the attack at Pearl Harbor, America's anxiety was heightened. Fearing an attack on the mainland, everyone was required by law to have their lights out.

One of the perks of being an air raid warden was that Dad would be allotted gas to drive around. That helped him get back and forth to work since the MGM studio was not within walking distance of his home. There were no cars being manufactured, auto plants were now making tanks, and gasoline was strictly rationed. As an air raid warden, he served both the war effort and Louis B. Mayer's MGM.

Rudd's MGM ID card

The war years at MGM were very good ones for Dad. Mayer ran the MGM studio as one big family. One of his top producers, David O. Selznick, was also his son-in-law. Perhaps Louis B. Mayer's biggest enjoyment in his later years were his two grandsons, Danny and Jeffrey Selznick.

Mayer was one of the best and most caring studio executives in Hollywood. He took great pride in MGM's Little Red Schoolhouse. It featured a gabled roof, a fireplace with a chimney, and a very picturesque front porch. MGM set designers were among the best in the industry and, supervised by the Los Angeles Board of Education, the building provided schooling for all of MGM's child actors for at least three hours a day. Among the students were Roddy McDowell and Elizabeth Taylor, the children in the *Lassie Come Home* cast. Some may have described Louis B. Mayer as rude and inconsiderate, but there was definitely another side to the man. That is what my father witnessed most often, the side that took very good care of him, and the side that loved Lassie.

After the phenomenal success of *Lassie Come Home* and its sequels, America was still a few years away from the dawn of the television age. With the war over, Americans began adjusting to new lives and new routines. Going to the movies remained as popular an American pastime as ever. Audiences loved their movie dogs and the studios knew who could best supply and train them. My father was finding steady employment in the motion picture industry, as well as a respected name for himself. Consequently, the Weatherwax kennels had to have a wide assortment of dogs to fit every studio need.

In addition to Lassie, other Weatherwax dogs had some interesting biographies of their own. Tramp was the dog who appeared in *The Fighting Sullivans* (1944). Tramp was retrieved from the pound as a young dog, although we could never be certain of his age. The remarkable thing was that, from the day we got him to when he ultimately died of cancer, he lived with us for over twenty years. That may not have been a record but, for a dog, it was a wonderfully long life.

United Artists released a movie titled *The Story of GI Joe* (1945), starring Burgess Meredith and Robert Mitchum. It was the life story of Pulitzer Prize winning war correspondent Ernie Pyle. Director William Wellman used Dad's dog, Shorty, throughout the movie. Shorty was a great character actor in Hollywood's dog world. He was cute and Dad could strip his fur forty different ways to make him look like a different dog in each new movie. *GI Joe* audiences were most likely unaware that they had also seen Shorty as Toots, in *Lassie Come Home*.

In 1952, Shorty auditioned for *Fearless Fagan*, a movie about a lion. Although the producers liked Shorty, they did not think his appearance fit the part. He needed to look a little less canine and a bit more feline. My father went home, got a stripping knife, and stripped the hair on Shorty until he looked like a little lion. The very next day he went back to the studio with Shorty and asked, "How about this dog?" Not realizing it was the same dog they had seen the day before they said, "We love him. He's perfect. Why didn't you show this dog to us to begin with?" My father just smiled and told them he had forgotten he had this dog in the kennel. They never knew the difference.

The success of Lassie also afforded my father some opportunities to perform himself. As he did for Mary Pickford many years earlier, Dad filled in as a stunt double for Peter Lawford in *Son of Lassie* (1945), the second in the Lassie movie series. When Peter was running into the woods, it was actually my father running with the dog. Since the director used a long distance shot, it was easier to have Lassie run with Dad because Lassie would eagerly follow him. He was built like Lawford so he got to relive the good old days when he was in front of the camera.

In 1947, Lassie hit the air waves as a regular radio program. Once again, my father got to show off his talent, this time as the program's narrator. He bought a recorder so he could check his voice and make sure everything sounded satisfactory. By this time, Pal sired a son to eventually take his place. Pal's son actually did most of the work in the last film, *The Painted Hills* (1951). Although he had problems with his vision, he performed on the radio show. The program was recorded in a studio next to where they were recording *The Frank Sinatra Show*. I thought my sister Jo Ann was going to faint when she first saw Frank.

That radio show was more fun to watch than making the movies. You would see one of the crew walking in a sandbox, making step sounds, while another was crinkling paper to make the sounds of something sizzling on the stove. I remember Hans Conried playing two different parts in one episode, and Lassie barking at him. *The Lassie Radio Show* ran for three years, bringing Lassie into the 1950s and the dawn of a brand new entertainment medium.

By 1951, the radio days were over for Lassie but movie work continued to keep the Weatherwax kennels busy. Director Christian Nyby needed a dog for his sci-fi thriller, *The Thing from Another World* (1951). Dad provided just the dog Nyby was looking for. This movie also introduced audiences to actor James Arness, who would soon morph from playing a very tall monster in the movies to U.S. Marshal Matt Dillon on television. Starring in what would become a long-running mega-hit TV Western called *Gunsmoke,* Arness would never have to look for another acting job for the rest of his life.

My father went to work on *Return of the Texan* (1952), directed by Delmer Daves. Daves was a powerhouse in Hollywood by then, with such directing credits as *Destination Tokyo* (1943), *Dark Passage* (1947), starring Bogart and Bacall, and as screenwriter for *The Petrified Forest* (1936), truly one of Hollywood's great classic films. It was during the filming of *Return of the Texan* that two memorable friendships developed. One was between my father and Dale Robertson, the other between me and a raccoon.

The film, which starred Robertson, Joanne Dru, and Richard Boone, called for a beagle. The dog's part wasn't big, but the job helped pay the bills. The script required the dog to interact with a raccoon. Dad decided to go to the pet store and get a raccoon so the dog could get used to one. He found a little guy with no hair and whose littermates apparently didn't make it. The pitiful little raccoon didn't look like he was much better off. They were taken away from their mother too soon and my father was extremely upset with the conditions in that pet store.

Luckily, we had a collie who just had puppies. Dad put the little raccoon in with the puppies. He was worried that the collie might not accept the little guy, but she treated him very well. She started licking and cleaning him, just like her own babies. When my father let the collie out, he noticed all the puppies still in place, but no raccoon. When he looked outside, he couldn't believe his eyes. There was the raccoon still clinging to the collie and feeding. I guess that's what raccoons do with their mother.

The raccoon used to put his tiny paws in our pockets and steal things while he was looking the other way. It was as if he thought that with that deception, no one would suspect he was stealing. That's how he earned the name Sneaky Pete.

An interesting thing about raccoons is that they wet their food before they eat it. We had a little bowl of water next to his food, and he would go back and forth, soaking his dry food and then eating it. I used to tease him by putting Jell-O or ice cream in his dish. He put his food in the water and watched it disappear. I had to smile when I saw his tiny hands thrashing around in the water wondering what happened to the food. I wasn't trying to be mean but it was such a huge temptation to have some fun with the little guy and watch how he reacted.

Sneaky Pete was attached to me, and only me. He liked to run up my leg to sit on my shoulder. Of course, when he got to be a thirty-pound animal, sitting on my shoulder became a bit of a problem. Sneaky used to sleep with me but, unfortunately, he liked to start playing about three o'clock in the morning. He would put his little hands in my ears and I'd brush him away. Then he would come right back. In the morning, he followed me around when I fed the dogs. As I put each pan down in front of the dog's door, Sneaky Pete would take a bite out of the food in the pan. The dogs didn't seem to mind. This routine continued all the way down the line with each pan and each dog.

I really loved that raccoon. He became a great part of my life. As with everything in the Weatherwax family, love was often elusive and attachments were considered useless distractions from the chaos of life. My parents often separated, and each time I was shuttled to another location until their latest tempest exhausted its fury. One of those times I spent in Virginia Beach, living with my sister while another hurricane Weatherwax ran its course. When I returned, I found that Sneaky Pete had not survived the storm. For some reason not known to me to this day, they decided that my most loving charge was no longer deserving of his wonderful life. It could have been a case of misery liking company but, when I returned home this time, Sneaky Pete was gone. I was told that he was given to another trainer. My heart was broken and, apparently, so was Sneaky Pete's. Locked in a crate, without anyone to play with in the middle of the night or a shoulder to climb on to survey the world, Sneaky Pete no longer found any joy in living. With his companion nowhere to be found, he died alone in his solitary confinement, the wire of a cage no substitute for the love of his boy. There isn't a single day in my life that I don't think of that little guy and want to tell him that I didn't abandon him, but was myself the victim of abandonment. He died in a cage without me, but forever lives in my heart.

After the last Lassie movie, *The Painted Hills* (1951), my father knew it was over for Lassie in feature motion pictures. He told my mother that it was a terrible movie and very amateurish. Nevertheless, Dad had the foresight to know that Lassie was still a big star and could still make him money beyond the box office, at shows and fairs across the country.

The Weatherwax accountant was a man named McDougall. He told my mother, who handled the family budget, that MGM owed my father $47,000. Mr. McDougall told Mom that if she took the money all at once, much of it would be taken in taxes. McDougall came up with a brilliant idea. He suggested that she take only $20,000 in a lump sum cash payment and negotiate the balance with MGM, offering to accept payment in full to include the Lassie name and the trademark. MGM thought they saw the writing on the wall. Lassie's movie life was at an end and no one could begin to imagine television as a very lucrative medium for filmed entertainment. MGM accepted the offer and Dad started the road shows. It was a circuitous route that would eventually end up in front of the television cameras.

Later, when Dad had successfully developed the TV show, he was notified that MGM was suing because they thought they owned the rights to Lassie. Dad knew that he'd bought them from MGM but was concerned that the representative did not have the official authority to make such a deal. He never heard from them again. Obviously, they checked into it and this representative did have that authority, but others at MGM were not aware of the agreement.

9

The Gravedigger's Lonely Job

ALTHOUGH LASSIE'S BRAND was fading, Dad realized that it would last for a while longer. Having secured the trademark from MGM, he prepared to take Pal on the road for live show appearances. My father felt he needed to make some money while the dog was still famous. Dad, like my grandfather, had a real knack for discovering opportunity wherever it could be found. For Pal, the success of the Lassie movies left him with a marketable commodity at fairs and rodeos, performing in twenty-minute shows across the country.

He also was aware that, unlike in the movies, Pal would not live forever. He had to ensure that this special line of collies would continue. In addition to Pal's fearless nature, which made him perfect for the distractions of the movie sets, his markings were truly something to behold. He had a pure white collar, with a white blaze going up his nose to a little above his eyes. Then, there were the all-white front legs going up to the collar. Pal, the original Lassie, was beautifully marked, as if Picasso had painted him.

Not everyone appreciated Lassie's beauty. Many of the personal appearances we did were collie club shows, and every time we would go to one, someone would come up to us and point out Lassie's flaws. It was true that Lassie, by the standards of a show collie, had many cosmetic flaws, the prominent blaze up his face being the most obvious.

Usually my father was paid by check for these appearances but, for some reason, one particular time they paid my father in cash at the show. I think he usually got $2500 per show. The money was in his pocket when one of the show people approached us and started to point out Lassie's imperfect markings. My father listened quietly, reached into his pocket, pulled out the big wad of cash, and said, "The difference between you and me is that you collect blue ribbons, I collect these green ones." He smiled and just walked away.

Dad did not breed until the current Lassie was getting close to retirement. He wanted Lassie bred to females with the white blaze down the head, all white mane, and all white front legs. These qualities were very hard to find. Also, our Lassies had broader heads than was considered the collie standard. We sometimes had to go through several litters to obtain the exact look. Often, Dad would turn to the well-known collie breeder, Ted Kattell, who lived in Vasquez Rocks.

Vasquez Rocks is located in an area that is today a national monument. In the second half of the nineteenth century, it was a place where the famous outlaw Tiburcio Vasquez hid out. He used this place because it had a very strange rock formation in which he could easily hide.

Tiburcio Vasquez was born in 1835 in a part of Mexico which is present-day Monterey, California. He was well-educated and spoke both English and Spanish. Tiburcio was handsome and literate, loved music, and played the guitar during those few times when he was not dancing. Women fell head-over-heels for this charming swashbuckler, who was also known to be a fan of romantic novels.

It did not take Tiburcio long to choose a different path for his life, one that would lead to prison and eventually his hanging. His life of crime included robberies, burglaries, cattle rustling, horse theft, and a prison break from San Quentin. If ever there was a western outlaw begging to be hanged, it was Tiburcio Vasquez. The sheriff finally caught up with him at a ranch located approximately two hundred yards from Sunset Strip in West Hollywood, near what is now Melrose Place. News of Tiburcio's arrest quickly spread. Female visitors flocked to his jail cell where he happily signed autographs for them.

On March 19, 1875, at the age of thirty-nine, Tiburcio met his fate. As he was about to ascend the scaffold, someone asked if he believed in an afterlife. He answered, "I hope so, because I will see all my sweethearts again!" I don't know how Ted Kattell found Tiburcio's hideout or why he decided to live there. Later on, when we were shooting the *Lassie* TV series, we used this area many times as a backdrop for the show.

I'll never forget the first time I went with my mother and father to see Ted Kattell. Before freeways, the trip took the better part of a day. After riding up a desolate road in the middle of nowhere, we arrived at a shack with an outhouse located behind it. When we got out of the car, a huge man came over, greeted us, and they all hugged. He said to my father, "I know why you're here. You want to breed Lassie." My father said, "Yes." Everyone went inside the shack for a while. It wasn't long before I had to go to the bathroom, so I went to Ted's outhouse.

The first thing I noticed was that it was filled with spiders. Even worse, the wooden seat with the hole in it was too high for me. I decided to go around to the back of the facility instead. Ted came running out, yelling, "Be careful. There's rattlesnakes out there." With that news floating in my head, I went back to the car and decided to suffer in silence. After what seemed like an eternity, my parents and Ted came out of the house. I heard Ted say to my father, "Well, Rudd, I guess you want to see them."

Ted let loose with a shrill whistle. Immediately, collies came out from everywhere. There were twenty coming from one mountain, ten more coming from another. Thirty emerged from a riverbed. There must have been a hundred collies coming to us from all over. I have never seen anything like that in my life. Ted's collies had a reputation of being strong and athletic, probably because they could roam the vast canyon rather than spend their days in pens. They climbed all over those mountains. If Dad had any doubts about breeding a successor for the original Lassie, they vanished as soon as he saw those collies come running at Ted's whistle, as if one hundred Lassies were coming home. Then Ted told my father, "Go ahead Rudd, find which one is best for you and let me know."

I always wondered why Ted lived isolated, alone with his dogs. I wanted to know more about this eccentric man with the hundred collies, the spiders in the outhouse, and the rattlesnakes out back. My mother said he was a scholarly man. He had that look about him too, like a professor. I asked why he lived like that. She told me that Ted lost his wife and daughter in a car accident, which may have affected his choices. Most people didn't know the man. He was really someone special, who would command your attention. Plus, he owned more collies than anyone I have ever known, before or since.

Collies galore!

Pal was definitely a hard act to follow. He had appeared in no less than seven Lassie movies, making him the fourth largest moneymaker for MGM, trailing only Mickey Rooney, Judy Garland, and Spencer Tracy. *Lassie Come Home* had grossed millions of dollars for the studio.

Pal had a son, one who actually worked as Lassie. He worked with Pal in the movie *The Painted Hills*, which was the last MGM Lassie movie. Pal also performed in this movie, but he was too old to do any of the physically demanding scenes. He was still good for close-up shots and had no problem doing his famous bark. Pal's son also was the only Lassie to appear in the radio show and was pictured on the cover of the book, *The Story of Lassie*.

Pal's son was partially blinded by botched eye surgery and this caused some major concerns. Once my brother Jackie left the gate open and the visually-challenged collie, discovering the open gate, merrily took off down the road to see the world. I thought it was a bad idea to have him in the front yard in the first place. We kept the other ones in the back yard specifically to prevent such a thing from happening. The back yard was double gated, one to let the dogs into the yard from the kennels, and another to pass through to leave the property.

When we discovered the collie missing, I rode around on my bicycle trying to find him. I didn't know where to look. Everybody was searching for him and eventually Dad put out a reward for our traveling Lassie, but he did not say who the animal really was. He just described the missing dog as a collie.

A neighbor saw the reward notice. They recalled seeing the dog and they brought the seriously injured animal over to our home. My father gave them five hundred dollars, which was a good reward in the 1950s.

Our newest Lassie had been hit by a car right in front of our house shortly after leaving the yard. Somehow, he had managed to crawl into somebody's car, not far from where we lived. When they returned to their car, they found him in the back seat. He was badly hurt. Our son of Lassie had been missing for two or three harrowing days. Although we were happy to get him back, the trauma of losing our dog and finding him badly injured was very upsetting. It was not a happy time at the Weatherwax home.

It was now apparent to my father that this dog would not be able to do the road shows because of his vision problems. Although Dad kept him and cared for him until he was very old, he had to be retired early. As a result, it became necessary to breed him. He sired a son, the grandson of Pal, and his name was Laddie. Dad started Laddie's training when he was between ten and twelve weeks old. At that age, they are not mature enough to learn to sit up or jump because their bodies have to develop. They are taught simpler things, like to come to you, tug on rags, play, and speak. This forms the basis for later training. Laddie went into training primarily to perform in road shows and with the hope he could be ready in case a movie job came around. My father's goal was to start a dog to work as Lassie at about two years of age. We had many other dogs in the kennel that got jobs, some were purebreds, but they were mostly mixed breeds. Most of the motion picture jobs called for mixed breeds we acquired from the pound. Dad picked most of them, with the occasional help from his other trainers. Dad would always make the final decision.

Frank Inn was pretty good at locating dogs. He found a great looking dog at the shelter and brought him into the kennel. It so happened that this dog was kenneled right next to Laddie, our future Lassie. What Frank didn't know was that the shelter dog had distemper. Out of forty dogs in the kennel, the one who became infected was Laddie. Sometimes we had to learn things the hard way, from experience. We certainly didn't know that the youngest dog in the kennel would be the most susceptible to the disease. We didn't know that you needed both puppy shots and a booster shot to really immunize a dog against distemper. We were learning some bitter lessons. After that, we quarantined our new dogs.

My bedroom was above the garage so that I was closer to the dogs I cared for. When Laddie got sick, he came to live with me as we tried to help him recover. I carried him up and down the steps four or five times every day so he could relieve himself.

At least once a week, Charles Reid, a well-known Hollywood veterinarian, came to our house. I'd always hold Laddie when we were treating him. Dr. Reid would draw blood from Laddie and inject him with different medicines. Every effort was made to try to cure him.

On one particular day, Dr. Reid told us that Laddie had deteriorated to the point that he would never have a good life and never be right. The distemper had caused Laddie to develop a central nervous system disease called chorea, a term I heard from the veterinarian. It made Laddie's limbs shake. The condition sounded to me like Korea, the war that was going on at the time, and that was the way I remembered to pronounce it.

Laddie somehow knew the day wasn't going according to his regular routine. He sensed that something was not right. Any hope that Laddie would recover vanished and he would only continue to suffer. Dr. Reid and my dad made the decision to put him to sleep.

Laddie died on the porch outside my bedroom. It was a sunny day. He had his head facing me and his back to the main house. I held the beautiful collie close to me while Dr. Reid euthanized him. I carried my beloved collie down the stairs to where Laddie would find his final resting place. I struggled with the same seventy pounds I had for months and, at first, did not understand why this was different. Then it suddenly struck me. I had always heard the term dead weight, and the difference was that Laddie was gone. There was no life, just the weight of the dog I had lost.

Grave digging is a lonely and solitary occupation. It always deals with sad endings. For a twelve-year-old boy, it was more than lonely, it was excruciating. Each shovelful of dirt removed from the ground seemed to build a pile of grief on top of my breaking heart.

I could hardly look at the lifeless body, carefully wrapped in a blanket off in the distance. My heart was breaking for all the innocence that was lost that day, when duty required that I transform from loving caretaker to lonely gravedigger. Laddie, trained to be the next Lassie, had lost his battle with distemper. He was only eighteen months old and had been living with me in the room above the garage. Now he was gone.

My heart was also breaking for my father, who could not face the reality of what had just happened. He left me alone to properly honor the remains of the dead. "Wrap him in his blanket," Dad instructed, "and never ever let any dirt touch his body."

I will never forget those very difficult and painful moments of my childhood. It's not that I wasn't used to hard tasks. "Everyone has to earn their keep," my father always told me. "No one gets a free ride!" Like his father before him, the man drilled this ethic into his children. He wove parables out of the stories of his youth, and used them to create a bible of life, now handed down to me, his son. With each patch of earth I removed from that gravesite, the parable of responsibility played over and over in my head. *Just keep digging,* I thought. *Dad says it has to be deep.*

10

Life After Laddie

MY FATHER HAD invested a great deal of time and effort into training Laddie. He was captivated by that dog and felt certain that he would be the perfect successor to Lassie. Having trained him since he was a two-month-old puppy, he found him eager and very intelligent. He felt that Laddie's training would have been finished when he was two years old, about the time he would assume the reigns of the Lassie legacy. Instead, Laddie went to his final resting place. Losing Laddie was a devastating blow to both me and my father. Both of us loved animals and were attached to our dogs, and these collies were in a category all by themselves.

I was able to care for Laddie full-time because I had just finished school for the summer. He was with me in my room for about six weeks until his death in late July or early August, 1952. The exact date eludes me now since the emotional toll it took on me erased any sense of time. For me, it was getting used to an empty room. For Dad, it was back to the drawing board. A new Lassie would need to be trained and ready for work. There were mouths to feed.

Dad now was in a panic because he suddenly had no collie to take on the road and, more importantly, to continue the line. Needing to find a replacement in a hurry, Dad paid Frank Inn a thousand dollars to find a collie that had the correct markings.

Dad had great faith that the only man who could produce the impossible was Frank Inn. He had no doubt that Frank would find the right dog in the shortest amount of time. Three weeks passed and still no successor could be found. Then a divine intervention occurred. One Sunday, as Frank prepared to go to church, he briefly scanned the newspaper hoping to find his treasure. He was dressed that morning in his expensive suit. On that memorable Sunday morning, he hit the jackpot. Someone had a collie needing a good home.

I don't know whether Frank made it to church that morning because he diverted his route in order to check out this collie. When he arrived at the owner's door, he was still dressed in his Sunday best. He sat patiently as the owner explained the situation. It seemed that the collie liked to bite. "He bit my son," said the owner, "but we don't want to take him to the pound. We just want to find a home for him." Frank couldn't believe his good fortune. The collie had a blaze that looked identical to Pal's. In fact, he was so close in appearance and personality to Pal that this wild-child may very well have been his descendant.

Frank wanted to close the deal before the owner changed his mind. Frank said, "I'll take him. I always wanted a collie like this." Frank was being a bit deceptive with these folks since he didn't tell them what he was really doing, which was searching for the next Lassie. However, the owner was a bit deceptive also. The collie did more than occasional biting and he was extremely aggressive. The dog wasted no time demonstrating to Frank just how difficult he was.

Frank hurriedly drove the dog home, knowing he was late for church. He quickly took the dog to his back yard, planning to deal with him after services. As Frank attempted to leave the yard, that collie proceeded to chase Frank. The dog caught up with him and tore Frank's sixty-nine dollar Jim Clinton suit. Sometimes the things you do literally come back to bite you. A piece of Frank's story may have been missing while negotiating with the owners, but now Frank was missing a piece of his suit.

When the collie arrived at our house he was hungry. I vividly remember that day when I fed him his first meal. He was in his pen and had just finished eating. He pushed the tray all the way to the other end of his kennel, trying to get that last morsel of food. I had no choice but to go into the pen and get that tray. When I did, the gate closed behind me. The next thing I knew, that huge dog was up on my chest, trying to bite me. I dropped the tray, unlatched the gate, and made a hair-raising escape. When I told my father what had just happened, he didn't believe a collie would be that aggressive. That was until he worked with the animal. He was in for a big surprise.

That collie absolutely did not care that he was in the presence of Rudd Weatherwax, Hollywood's top dog trainer. That did not matter in the least. If he could demolish Frank Inn's suit and terrorize the trainer's son, attacking the trainer was certainly not out of the question, which is exactly what he did. Even for Dad, this dog was going to be a challenge.

No one ever knew when a Lassie had to be retired or died. Lassie lived forever. That was part of the image my father created. Consequently, we never told the public that the Lassie line had been broken.

The new Lassie would have to learn his acting skills in a short amount of time. He also needed a serious personality change before coming into contact with a cast and crew. Dad had his work cut out for him. There was also a nagging worry in the back of my father's mind that just would not go away. For the second time in his career, acquiring a Lassie dog required deception. Dad wondered if the previous owners would recognize their dog, especially later when the prospect of Lassie appearing on television became a possibility. Sometimes, what goes around comes around. At least this time, the owners were a bit deceptive themselves. Frank Inn's tattered Sunday suit was testimony to that.

11

The Fortune Teller

AFTER THE MOVIES it was not clear what would become of Lassie. The road shows would make some money and we still had our core business supplying other dogs. It was during this time that my mother went to a fortune teller. In addition to what he told her, the one thing that caught her attention was that the room was full of clocks with no hands. They were all ticking, but none of them gave a clue as to what time it was. The effect left a lasting impression on her, as did the cryptic message the fortune teller was about to convey.

He told her that she was going to make money in a "commodity not yet known." He didn't tell her what that commodity was. As is always the case, the crystal ball was long on mystique and short on specifics. My mother was bright enough to know what a commodity was, but the ones she was familiar with were wheat and corn. As later events unfolded, she realized what the man was talking about. The commodity was television.

Dad never really thought about the new medium of television. He focused his time on his business supplying dogs to the studios and training the new collie for personal appearances. Then my father met

Robert Maxwell. Maxwell's wife had just inherited a lot of money and he saw potential in this new medium of television. He thought we could make Lassie into a TV show. The deal was that if my father did the pilot for nothing, he would receive 10% of the show if it sold. My father accepted the deal with one caveat. He told Maxwell that Frank Inn had to be paid along with any other expenses incurred.

During the early days of television, shows were not sold to networks as they are today. You first had to have a sponsor. Bob Maxwell had to go to New York to try to sell the show. Although he financed the trip on his own, he was soon running out of cash. For weeks he was unsuccessful in finding a sponsor. Convinced that he had an idea worth something, he persisted, staying at cheap hotels and picking up match books at The Plaza so people would think he was staying at an expensive hotel. Despite Maxwell's best efforts, time and money were running out with no sponsors secured. The project was in danger of complete collapse. Desperate, Maxwell called my father and asked if he could tender a ten-thousand-dollar loan. Dad had only five-thousand, so he asked his brother Frank for the balance. Frank refused, convinced that Maxwell was a swindler and had already stolen money. Frank would not contribute to what he believed to be a scam. Dad next turned to his friend, Jimmy Casey. Years earlier, Jimmy had been blackballed by the industry for reasons connected to personal problems. He asked Jimmy for the five-thousand dollars and Jimmy gave it to him. That loan turned out to be the thing that made the *Lassie* TV show possible.

On his last day in New York, with his last dollar, as Maxwell made plans for a long trip home with empty pockets, he made one last stop. He went to the Campbell Soup Company. They loved the idea and agreed to sponsor the show. The *Lassie* show was saved by an ostracized production manager and a can of soup. To show his gratitude to Jimmy Casey for the loan that saved the show, Dad had him hired as an assistant director. To show his gratitude to Campbell Soup, he gave them a hit TV show.

Needless to say, the rest is history. The *Lassie* series was an instant success as millions of television viewers from coast to coast tuned in to find out what was happening with the Miller Family. The cast was terrific, with Jan Clayton as Jeff's mother Ellen, George Cleveland as Gramps, Tommy Rettig as Jeff, and America's favorite collie. Lassie had no problem adapting to the new medium of television.

The actors who would become Lassie's television family were a story in themselves. Jan Clayton was already a big star on Broadway and was an important figure to have in the cast as she had just finished *Carousel.* George Cleveland was a well-known character actor, and Tommy was the top child star at the time. The studios wanted big stars to increase the odds of success. The three actors fit that description perfectly.

Jan Clayton spent a lot of time at our house. Ours was a drinking house and Ms. Clayton fit right in. Tragically, her teenage daughter was killed in a traffic accident. After that, her drinking increased as she dealt with her loss.

George Cleveland was a gentleman and carried a flask in his pocket, a natural for the Weatherwax home. Like Ms. Clayton, George came over to the house frequently. He was always impeccably dressed in his three piece suits. He had a meticulously groomed moustache that gave him the look of a statesman and the flask was discreetly placed.

I could still picture George sitting in a chair and telling stories. Both on and off screen he came across as a grandfather. My real grandfather, Walter, passed away when I was too young to remember much about him. In the early 1950s, I was old enough to enjoy George Cleveland's stories. They would capture my attention and he didn't mind talking to a child.

Of all the original cast members, my friendship with Tommy Rettig was unique. Our bond was forged in the crazy world of Hollywood and would last until his death. Tommy was only five-feet-four-inches tall. He was a very young looking twelve-year-old when he first came to the ranch to audition for the role of Jeff Miller. The tryouts included Lee Aaker, who would later be cast as Rusty in the *Rin Tin Tin* television series. When the session was over, Tommy was offered the role. While Tommy got to work with the famous collie, Lee got to work with the famous German shepherd.

Tommy was a major child star by the time he was cast to play Jeff. He had several feature films in his acting resume. Before filming of the TV show began, my father wanted Tommy to build a rapport with Lassie. Dad told Tommy's mother that he needed him to spend a couple of weeks at our house. Tommy shared my bedroom above the garage. We were the same age and in the same grade in school.

Tommy was very closely supervised by his mother. As the family's breadwinner, he was never able to see or do much like other kids our age. Whenever he came over to the house we'd walk down to see my neighbors and smoke a cigarette. For those few moments, he could feel like an ordinary kid. As we grew older, we would go cruising with my friends who owned cars. It was the era of James Dean and *Rebel Without a Cause* (1955).

We would sometimes have a beer and do things which Tommy's mother would certainly not approve. Fortunately, she never discovered what was going on. My father and mother didn't keep track of me the way Tommy's mother kept track of him. She tried to protect him around the clock. Despite her persistent vigilance, she never dared to say no to my father. If he wanted Tommy to come over to spend time with Lassie, then that was how it was to be. Dad would go out into the yard to train him to walk with Tommy or give him a kiss, and soon they got used to working with each other. Unlike my other friends, Tommy was allowed to go out in the yard and play with Lassie. He had free run with all our dogs. Lassie always knew when he was there.

In 1954, when Tommy and I were around thirteen years old, we went into town to see a movie. Outings to the theater were always fun and we both looked forward to them. On this particular day, the theater had a poster display advertising one of the coming attractions. The movie was titled *River of No Return* (1954) and it starred Robert Mitchum and Marilyn Monroe. It also starred none other than Tommy Rettig. All three of the stars were pictured on the poster. It didn't take long for a group of teenage girls to recognize Tommy. Within seconds, they were all over him. He protested, "Don't get on me. This guy's father owns Lassie." They didn't care, all they wanted was him. We did enjoy the movie, although I have long forgotten what it was. What I do recall is that when the previews began, there on the big screen was my friend. As I watched him standing alongside Robert Mitchum and Marilyn Monroe, it finally dawned on me that Tommy was a major star. He told me later that Marilyn Monroe was a nice lady. He saw her as a child would. We never talked about his work on the *Lassie* show. My father owned Lassie and Tommy worked on the show. It was our time together that gave us pleasure.

As a young adult living in his own apartment, Tommy once told me, "If it weren't for you, I wouldn't have had a life when I was younger. You provided me the only normalcy I ever knew. My life consisted simply of studios and school. I'd come to your house and hang out with your friends, smoke cigarettes, drink a beer, and do things that a teenager would do." He was very happy with those times we shared together, and neither of us ever forgot them.

Despite the heavy work load as a child star, Tommy ended up with very little money. His mother had difficulty wisely managing the money he earned. The part of his salary she was required to set aside for his future somehow ended up needing to be spent on other things.

Monthly expenses in the home of a superstar could be staggering at times. His mom no doubt did her best to look after his interests but I think she became overwhelmed and fell short.

She told him she was going to use his savings to buy him a home. Tommy authorized the expenditure and when he became an adult, he moved in. Imagine how surprised he was when deputy sheriffs arrived on his doorstep to repossess his house. It turned out that it hadn't been completely paid for.

Tommy was never bitter. The lovable boy you saw on the screen was the same in real life. He had a big heart and always displayed a positive outlook on life. He certainly loved his mom and the love was unconditional. He never said a cross word about his mother. She was his mom and nothing could break that bond. Nothing else was that important, not even a house.

When the opening scenes for the television series were being filmed, Dad was in Mexico working on the movie *Hondo* (1953) with John Wayne. As much as he wanted, he could not be on the set of the new television series. Frank Inn covered for Dad. Far different from a kinescope recording of a studio stage show, the *Lassie* pilot was filmed in some gorgeous locations, including the state of Washington.

The script called for the show to open with Lassie running into frame, jumping onto a rock, surveying his world. For years, that was the scene viewers saw as the show opened. Later, after Tommy left the show, the opening was changed to Lassie hearing Timmy's call, running and jumping over the fence. By then, television sets were more prevalent and that opening became the one most viewers identify with.

The night of the *Lassie* show premiere, everyone came to our house to watch it. My father's brother Frank and his wife Connie, my parents, my sister, and I all gathered for the big event. My father intended to make Lassie raising his paw at the end of the show his trademark. It was my mother's idea to assure that my father received credit. At the end of the show, Lassie lifted his paw and the credits read "Lassie is owned and trained by Rudd Weatherwax." Connie jumped up from the chair and went ballistic. I thought there was going to be a real brawl that night. Frank was pacing around with a cigar in his mouth and said to my father, "This isn't right." I quietly slipped out of the house as they started fighting and went to my room above the garage.

They never got over that. Frank and Connie thought it should say Lassie was trained by both Rudd and Frank. That wasn't going to happen. Dad was never going to do that because he was not trained by both of them. They were business partners but Lassie was owned and trained by Dad. Frank didn't train any of those dogs.

While Lassie had a long running TV series, Frank was supposed to take on the other jobs the business was offered. After a few years of the *Lassie* series, Frank decided he wasn't going to work anymore and gave up all his dogs. A lawsuit was then initiated by my father. He felt that since Frank decided not to work, he should not continue to receive 50% of the business profits. Their respective wives got involved, Dad's third wife, Betty, and Frank's wife, Connie. They both had children from prior marriages and wanted them taken care of. My parents were divorced by that time and my mother took Frank's side in court. She kept all the business records and was able to show that there was a precedent that my father paid Frank 50%. The lawsuit ended with Dad holding on to 60% of the business while Frank's cut would only be 40%. At the time of either of their deaths the business would revert back to 50% each.

Dad and his brother, Frank, did not speak for four or five years after the lawsuit. They only reconciled at the end of their lives.

During those first three years, the Lassie TV production company had been humming along. It took approximately three days to film a thirty-minute episode, working ten hours a day, six days a week. This routine went on for nine months each year with a hiatus in the summer. The new medium of television absolutely dominated the lives of the men, women, and children who were fortunate enough to be regulars in a popular TV series.

Nothing lasts forever, however. After three years, only George Cleveland and Lassie were looking forward to a fourth season. Jan Clayton wanted to return to her stage roots on Broadway. Tommy was fifteen and getting too old for the part and was looking for a change in his personal and professional life. He had faithfully performed with Lassie in 116 episodes, devoting most of his waking hours to the show. For Tommy Rettig, the oppressive workload of the *Lassie* series was a huge hindrance to any type of social life he might have envisioned for himself as a teenager.

The search for Tommy Rettig's replacement was on. Jon Provost auditioned for the part and things could not have gone better for him. He loved animals and had absolutely no fear of them. When he arrived at our house, he did not hesitate. Jon sprinted over to Lassie and gave him a big hug. Dad issued a command and Lassie gave Jon a kiss on the face. Jon was not acting. He smiled in absolute delight. It was real. In fact, it was love at first sight. At that moment, you saw a boy and a dog, both interacting with each other naturally. Tommy had a fine replacement and could go on with his life. Jon had everything he needed to make a smooth transition for the millions of viewers who tuned in to the show each Sunday.

Despite his leaving the show, Tommy and I remained very close friends for the rest of his life. There were gaps in our relationship, when he lived somewhere else and I didn't see him for two or three years, but we always kept in touch. In 1996, Tommy moved to Marina del Rey and was on the verge of earning a comfortable income as a brilliant software engineer. Suddenly, at the age of 54, a heart attack took him from us and we lost one of the world's finest people.

A funeral service was held for Tommy at a restaurant in Marina del Rey. Roger Clinton, the President's brother, and I gave eulogies. I had a friend, who made signs professionally, prepare a banner in honor of Tommy which was hung at the restaurant for the occasion. It read:

"LASSIE LOST HIS BEST FRIEND"

The letter "I" in friend was dotted with a heart which was broken. I had the sad responsibility of taking Tommy's ashes out to sea on my boat, La Sea. Tommy's sons and Roger were there as we spread his ashes over the ocean. The wind blew some back and we all inhaled a few, so I always say that Tommy will be part of us all now. The last time I cried when someone passed away was for Tommy. I still miss my childhood friend.

The cutthroat entertainment business operates on a cost basis. Time is money and production companies hate to lose either, and it was no different with the *Lassie* series. Fearing that a man in his late 60's might cost the production company money should he pass away during filming, they had George Cleveland film his death scene ahead of time. My father came home afterwards and remarked that it really put some reality in his life. The scene was put in the can and saved as insurance.

The *Lassie* production company cashed in on that insurance just as the fourth season was to begin. Just as the scriptwriters were gearing up to create stories involving new cast members, George Cleveland, now seventy-one years old, decided to use some of his precious time off to relax and play a round of golf. He never finished the game. Suffering a fatal heart attack on the golf course, George Cleveland died on July 15, 1957.

Lassie now had a new best friend in Jon Provost and a new family with Cloris Leachman & Jon Shepodd as Jon's parents. Ms. Leachman, not wanting to play second fiddle to a dog, left after one year. Feeling that both parents had to be replaced, Jon Shepodd was let go and June Lockhart and Hugh Reilly became Timmy's new parents. They expected that the show would get a flood of letters protesting the replacements but, to their amazement, there was not one letter. Over the years, the cast and setting of the Lassie series would change. What never changed was Lassie and the extraordinary man training him, Rudd Weatherwax.

Bob with three of Lassie's boys, Tommy Rettig, Will Estes, and Jon Provost

Cast members weren't the only ones leaving the enormously successful TV production. Bob Maxwell, who was producing the show, wanted to sell while it was still on top. Most shows didn't last on television more than five years. He found Jack Wrather, who was willing to purchase it. Bob Maxwell told my father that Wrather would not do this show with Dad getting 10%. He told him that Wrather wanted 100%. My father felt that he had no choice, so he agreed. He would work for a trainer's salary and Lassie would get fifteen hundred dollars a week. This deal was set "in perpetuity." Unfortunately, my father didn't use a lawyer and didn't know what those words meant. In his case, they indicated that his salary would remain the same, basically forever. For the next fifteen years, Lassie was one of the cheapest shows produced on television. Wrather made money hand over fist while, comparatively speaking, my father made next to nothing. It was the MGM situation all over again.

Toward the end of the series, encouraged by his third wife Betty, Dad went on strike for a year leaving Sam and me to work Lassie. He finally got more money, but hated being away and wanted to know what happened on the set each day. I was always careful about what I told him because, good or bad, he would get upset. It was a delicate balance because Lassie meant everything to my father.

As other actors got raises, Dad's salary did not change. Animals never got residuals, even superstars like Rin Tin Tin and Lassie. Only human actors would eventually qualify for residuals, thanks to the Screen Actors Guild. These were payments most often associated with the entertainment industry. They were based on the premise that a work of art such as a song, movie, or TV show could generate income far beyond its original performance.

Most shows do not make a profit for the producer until they go into syndication. Lassie made a profit right from the start. Production costs were much lower. There were very few makeup or wardrobe people, and cast and crew members were minimal. The production depended mostly on the trainer, his assistants, and the dog.

Despite the fact that the producers had a lopsided deal with him, my father was always concerned that they would try to replace him. He desperately wanted to do the show. It was his whole life. When a person has that frame of mind, they are thankful for whatever they can get. Everyone was satisfied at the time.

After my military service, I worked on every remaining episode of *Lassie*. Driving home each day, all that my father would talk about were the shots we completed. I used to say, "Dad, we do this all day long. Do we have to talk about it on the way home?" The answer was, "Yes." Every day during that drive, my father went over each and every detail. On weekends, he watched the show intensely and critiqued everything he did. He always felt he could find ways to make things better. That's how much he cared about it.

No one ever really knew how much my father was involved in actually creating Lassie. He never took credit for training the dog. All he cared about was working his star dog. He put the dog out front, remaining out of the spotlight. People often remarked, "You must spend a lot of time training that dog, Mr. Weatherwax." "Why, no," he would say, "Lassie is a very smart dog. He does that on his own. Anyone can work him."

It was Rudd Weatherwax who built the Lassie name and created the superstar image for those collies. They were always presented as perfect stars. He never allowed photos to be taken of the dogs in embarrassing situations. No one ever knew that it was Rudd Weatherwax who created the live version of Lassie, who performed some amazing feats but did so in a way that was still believable to the audience. Jack Wrather approached Dad with an idea to do a show with Lassie and one of his other properties, Superman. Dad stubbornly refused since Superman was clearly a fictional character from another planet. Lassie, on the other hand, was an ordinary farm dog with extraordinary instincts. Some things she did may have been unlikely but not impossible. That was all part of the image Dad nurtured.

Pal jumping through Rudd's arms.

They say that a genius is no different from the rest of us except in one major way. A genius has a vision. It is a vision of how to attain the unattainable, to make possible the impossible. The Wright Brothers and Glenn Curtiss showed the world that man could fly. Philo Farnsworth showed the world that radio programs could also be seen with his television device. Rudd Weatherwax taught dogs how to become professional actors just like their human counterparts. These men all had a vision. They changed the world in which we now live. True geniuses, one and all.

Spook preparing to board a flight with Silky.

12

Lassie Behind the Scenes

THE STORIES OF the people behind the scenes of the *Lassie* show were as interesting as the show itself. Of course there was my father, the gifted trainer who was his owner. Part of his talent lay in the ability to make people think the dogs were performing completely on their own. People honestly believed that we were there only to feed and brush that intelligent collie and drive him home at night. Driving was a skill that no Lassie ever acquired, although one of them did once climb into the cockpit of a military jet.

The image of Lassie as a fearless, heroic, and almost human dog continued to grow. Like his human counterparts, Lassie learned to always turn towards the camera, never away from it. When deciding which direction to go, Lassie would look to the right, pause for a couple of beats, look to the left, appear to make up his mind, and move off. Some of the studio executives thought our collie was born with these skills. To our detriment, many people, including those with whom we had to negotiate salary matters, also believed the myth. I can hardly imagine that many of those high-powered executives really thought that a dog could be taken to a movie set and left to perform on his own. Maybe they were using their feigned ignorance as a negotiating tool.

From trains to military jets, Lassie knew how to travel first class.

Sam Williamson was one of my father's assistants. Unlike Frank Inn's flamboyant nature, Sam was content doing his job quietly behind the scenes. When I first joined my father as an assistant, he was very hard on me. He had always envisioned my brother, Jackie, becoming his successor, a hope that by this time had all but vanished. The first few years I worked for him, my father tried to get me to quit. He would tell everybody on the set that I didn't know what I was doing. He belittled me all the time, like a drill sergeant in basic training. Sam Williamson was instrumental in helping me deal with my father day after day in our working relationship. After work, Sam went over the day's production in order to give me an understanding of the requirements of the work. With Sam's help, I steadily got better at my job. Without Sam, I don't think I would have survived those early days in my career. My father was not an easy man to work with. He was a perfectionist in a hard business. Sometimes when the pressure would catch up with him he would take it out on Sam and me. It is not a business for the faint of heart.

Sam suffered from severe chronic pain that nothing could ease. After a life of suffering, Sam chose to end it to escape the pain. He had enormous respect for my father and knew that Dad hated suicide because of his first wife. Sam waited until Dad passed away and, a few days later, took his own life. He left me his Jack Russell terrier, whom I renamed Sam in his honor. He was one of the dogs used in the movie *Michael* (1996).

Bill Beaudine Jr. was the production manager for the Lassie TV show. His father, William Beaudine Sr. was a director and a pioneer in the earliest days of the California motion picture industry. In 1909, at the age of seventeen, he was working at Thomas Edison's Biograph studios. Six years later, he was alongside D.W. Griffith as assistant director on the epic silent film, *Birth of a Nation* (1915). His first talkies were several of the Max Sennett comedy shorts. He worked for the Metro Company and the Goldwyn Company before both merged into MGM. Bill Beaudine Sr. was off to a great start in the big leagues of Hollywood.

Over time, his A-List movie career derailed and Bill Beaudine Sr. was consigned to low-budget productions. He paid his bills with forgettable fare like *Windbag the Sailor* (1936). His days of working with Hollywood icons like Mary Pickford were now just part of his past.

In the low-budget film world, Beaudine Sr. quickly learned that survival depended on valuing quantity over quality. To pay the bills at the end of the month, you had to crank out as many films as possible. Artistic quality and production value had to fall by the wayside and Bill Beaudine Sr. became a master of slapping projects together as rapidly as possible. He had mastered the practice of finishing a project on time within budget and producers loved him.

Old habits stretching back decades are hard to break. Bill Sr.'s propensity for disregarding artistic merit continued on the *Lassie* Show. He churned out episodes like a factory assembly line. As long as the actors didn't trip and fall running around the set, everything else was acceptable. The production budgets and deadlines were all that mattered.

Bill Beaudine Sr. was a man of stature, maybe close to six feet tall. He had big front teeth, bushy eyebrows, and a Charles de Gaulle nose. When I worked with him, his hair was a distinguished gray and he was always well-dressed. Sam Williamson used to refer to him as William X. Crawley, a reference to a pseudonym Bill Sr. used when directing some of those early films. The rest of the crew referred to him as "The Old Man."

Bill Sr. had a great sense of humor and loved to irritate my father. He noticed that we always rewarded Lassie after each scene. Lassie, like the other professional actors, wanted to be compensated for his work and food was his currency. We always carried with us a little bag filled with small pieces of meat. I had one, Sam Williamson had one, and my father had one. Whoever was involved in the shoot with Lassie rewarded him. If it turned out to be a three person shot, all three of us rewarded him. As a result, Beaudine Sr. started calling Lassie "the meat hound." He'd yell, "Bring in the meat hound!" Bill Beaudine Sr. became a master of pushing my father's buttons. Jon Provost wasn't a huge fan of Beaudine Sr. either. Every time he directed he insisted that Jon wear a little straw hat. He thought Jon looked cute in it, but Jon hated that hat.

Beaudine Sr. had a very peculiar habit. As the actors said their lines, his lips would move with the dialogue. It was more fun to watch him than what was in front of the camera. He would say, "I want Lassie to snarl." Dad would have Lassie snarl and Beaudine snarled along with him with his big teeth showing. He was a show within himself. We should have reversed the camera and filmed him.

William Beaudine Sr. was only one of the directors to work on the *Lassie* show. Directors rotated and some were better than others. Jack Hively had a habit of shooting from three different angles, as he was rumored to be short on editing skills. He found it difficult to gauge what shots the editor needed to stitch the show together in post-production. To compensate for this shortcoming, Jack would shoot a master shot from Position A, and another from Position B. Nobody was that tedious with master shots. It was referred to in the industry as "over-shooting" and drove the crew crazy. Jack had good reason to worry. If a director came up short on footage needed for a good edit, then there was no way to go back and get those shots. Any director leaving gaps for the editor would not last long in the hiring rotation. I always pictured Jack lying awake at night, obsessing about the day's shoot and wondering if he got all the shots he needed.

Chris Nyby was a top quality director. In addition to the *Lassie* Show, he later did an episode of *Run Joe Run* with me. His list of credits made Beaudine Sr. seem like a minor leaguer in the directing world. Chris was a powerhouse in the world of classic TV shows, especially Westerns. Anyone who watched *Bonanza, Gunsmoke, Rawhide,* or *The Roy Rogers Show* was exposed to Chris's work. The non-Western TV fans were also entertained with his work on *Mayberry RFD, Perry Mason,* and *The Streets of San Francisco,* to name a few. Chris also shared in the story of the crossed career paths my father and I shared. In one of those twists of fate, Chris directed the horror movie, *The Thing from Another World* (1951). Years later, I would work with director John Carpenter on the remake, *The Thing* (1982).

Chris was a heavy hitter when it came to the *Lassie* show directors. He created high quality productions. Having been an editor himself, he knew what was needed, would never over-shoot, and brought the episodes in on time.

In the 1950s, Texas oil millionaire Jack Wrather decided to look to Hollywood for some investment opportunities. He formed a production company and started acquiring rights to various entertainment properties. As a Texan, Jack had no problem putting *The Lone Ranger* at the top of his acquisition list along with the now successful *Lassie* show. In 1956, when Bob Maxwell was ready to leave the project, Wrather was a willing buyer.

Bonita Granville Wrather, an Academy Award nominated actress and wife of Jack Wrather, was entrusted with the role of producer. She could not have been happier. She loved the *Lassie* show. Bonita was a very kind and gracious person. Once while on location in Big Bear, I got very sick and needed to see a doctor. There was no one available to take me so Bonita told me to get in her car. She not only drove me herself, but also waited for me and drove me back to the set. Thoughtful people were not that common in the production-obsessed world of Hollywood, but she was the exception.

When I was first hired to be one of my father's assistants, the production was on hiatus. During the down times between seasons, the studio booked publicity tours for Lassie. It was crucial to the success of the program for Lassie to get out and mingle among the fans. My father wasn't into publicity tours, so he would send his senior assistant, Sam Williamson, with me as Sam's assistant. Sam was in charge since I was new on the job.

One of our venues was the 1962 World's Fair in Seattle. Jon Provost was in Seattle with us, along with his studio social worker. There were no performances, but we did participate in a number of interviews and press conferences. At that time, Lassie was a dog we nicknamed Spook. He was in the opening of the *Lassie* show walking down the road with Jon Provost.

Spook earned his nickname on his first day on the set. In a scene where June Lockhart was to come into the kitchen, Lassie was supposed to come in behind her. While shooting the scene, a lamp fell and nearly hit him. The crash terrified him and, after that mishap, he associated the incident with June Lockhart. He was afraid of one of the show's main stars. My father tried letting Lassie stay with June in her dressing room to see if he could break him of the fear but it didn't work. We tried having the dog sit as soon as he came into the kitchen, but we didn't realize that Spook could move while he was sitting. The cameraman would say, "Bob, we don't know what's happening but the dog is moving out of the shot." He was doing everything he could to get away. To resolve this, my father decided that whenever we shot a scene in the kitchen, Lassie would come in and immediately go and lay under the stove. That became his place where he felt safe.

About four or five years before I started working on the show, Jon Provost had come on as Lassie's new master. Jon was a nice little boy but did have a mischievous side. The hotel's executive rooms were usually on the top floors and Jon liked to hit every button on the elevator on the way up. We ended up stopping at every floor, and there were at least twenty-nine floors between us and the press conference. That was when Sam looked Jon directly in the eyes and told him, "I will kill you if you do that again!" Jon smiled, turned around, and continued pressing the elevator buttons. He knew that Sam would do no such thing.

During the press conference, Spook saw something that frightened him and he ran underneath a table. Sam, being quick-witted and used to Spook's idiosyncrasies, said, "Get under the table, Lassie. Get under there." Members of the press were amazed and amused. They thought Spook was acting right on cue. Sam told them, "He does that to keep out of your way. He's taught to get under a table in a crowd. That way, nobody steps on him." Sam was on top of his game that day, especially when you consider that the press conference took place less than an hour after Sam threatened Jon Provost with his life.

13

Lassie the Celebrity

AFTER *LASSIE COME Home* became a hit, Pal had to travel to promote the movie. People were beginning to take advantage of commercial airlines, abandoning the trains for planes. Lassie was no different, but just as the railroads insisted that he ride as cargo, the airlines wanted to put him in the luggage compartment. A decompressing luggage bay could create much more havoc than a crate of unripened apples. Lassie could have died and my father wouldn't allow that. Dad said, "I don't have another one of these dogs and I wouldn't do it anyway because he's my dog." MGM President Louis B. Mayer agreed. He realized that the studio had a very valuable commodity in Lassie. The dog was one of the superstars in the MGM universe.

When Mayer found out that the airline wanted to transport Lassie as cargo, he contacted his friend, Howard Hughes, who just happened to own TWA. He quickly agreed with Mayer and Lassie became the first dog in history to fly as a passenger on an airplane. Years later we were able to upgrade Lassie to first class. The airline officials did it, no questions asked, putting his name on the airline ticket as a passenger.

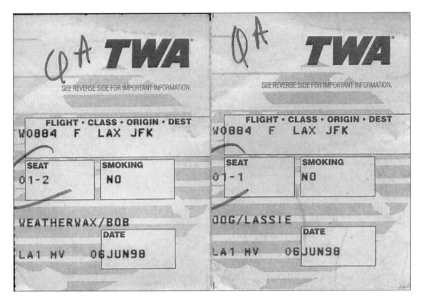

Lassie flies first class.

Flying wasn't the only hazard my dad and Lassie had to overcome. As people kept asking for Lassie's autograph, Dad would dip Pal's paw in ink. Removing the ink from his fur was time consuming and my father was astute enough to realize that this was not going to be a passing fad. It was obvious that Lassie had captured America's heart and it looked like the love affair was going to be a lasting one. My father had an imprint made of Pal's paw from which he created a wooden stamp. I am always reminded of the legion of Lassie fans whenever I look at the original stamp, which I still use to this day.

At one point, Louis B. Mayer wanted the MGM lion replaced with Lassie but he was outvoted by his partners on that idea. Mayer really loved Lassie, as well as the millions of dollars that the dog had brought in to MGM. He did gain one concession. In one of the later Lassie movies, the MGM logo came up and we saw Lassie and heard his bark in place of the roar of the MGM lion.

Lassie held immense public relations potential for the studios. It was only natural that crowds would thrill to Lassie arriving in a limo and jumping out like James Cagney or Joan Crawford.

Lassie arriving in a limo to greet his adoring fans.

In the years following the end of the movies, with the Hollywood days over, Rudd and Pal mesmerized crowds with a live twenty-minute show. It offered fans an opportunity to meet the legendary canine movie star and enjoy a program of various acts designed to display Lassie's talents. Throughout the years, he performed in the stage shows across the country and they became quite an attraction.

As an example, we reenacted a scene from one of the movies in which Lassie was poisoned by the villain and was struggling to get home. He walked slowly then crawled, pretending to be so weak that he would lay on his side, still trying to move. I then came on the stage to pick up the stricken animal. Lassie was absolutely limp, lying on his side, which is a very difficult thing to get a dog to do. I'd carry him around to show that he was limp, then put him back down. Then the announcer would say, "But all's well that ends well," and Lassie would jump up and bound over my back, much to the surprise of the smiling and laughing audience. Then we would bring out the villain who caused it all, and Lassie would attack him. We told the kids, "Now, the louder you scream, the more he's going to attack." They loved to watch Lassie get his revenge and screamed at the top of their lungs. Once the stuntman had earned his wages for the day, Dad would go out onstage and call Lassie off. The villain would try to walk off the stage but he still had a dog hanging onto his leg. At the end we would all come out and have Lassie take three bows, hold up his paw, and wave goodbye.

Another act we performed required a little girl to come up from the audience and pretend that she was leaving without finishing her homework. Lassie went after her, took her arm, and brought her back. Another popular trick was to tell the audience that offstage there was another dog who fought with Lassie in a movie and he's a pretty ferocious dog, so we're not sure we should really bring him out. We then sent Lassie backstage and he returned with a leash in his mouth, pulling a meek little terrier, Mel, Lassie's traveling companion. The audience laughed and got a really big kick out of it. Mel then stayed out on the stage and imitated Lassie crawling on the ground. Before the laughter subsided, Mel ran to a barrel, started rolling it, and began to dance. He then twirled around a couple times before I made a loop out of my arms. Once he saw that loop, Mel had a lot of fun jumping through it repeatedly. The audience cheered.

Lassie takes a leap of faith.

There were some tricks which were extremely popular with the kids. Two lucky children were selected to come on stage. They lined up along a table and we had them bend so their backs would be flush with the table. The announcer would warn the volunteers, "You better be careful because someone once looked up and lost his head." I stood on the same side as the kids, with Lassie on the opposite side. When I called him, Lassie jumped on the table and leaped over the children. He would fly through the air and I'd catch him in my arms.

Lassie keeping America beautiful.

Lassie's fans came from all walks of life. While most actors appeal to a certain type of audience, Lassie's fans ranged from children to adults, rich and poor, and everyone in between. They all loved Lassie. He had a much wider appeal than most actors. Even the White House was drawn to the Lassie mystique.

Jack Wrather had a lot of political power and Bonita, Jack's wife, served on numerous presidential committees. In the series, whenever Lassie visited a national park, he was trained to pick up litter and put it in the trash can. He was the park rangers' best friend. Lady Bird Johnson saw that and wanted Lassie as her spokesdog for the anti-littering campaign, "Keep America Beautiful."

Lassie met the First Lady and the Secretary of Agriculture at the White House. Dad and I were there with Bob Bray, who starred as one of the park rangers on the TV series. We posed Lassie with Smokey the Bear who was caged behind the White House, patiently waiting for his photo op.

14

The World Beyond Television

"COME ON. I want you to meet somebody." I was ten years old when I first heard those words, and each time my father spoke them I was about to experience one of the most fascinating moments of my life. Lassie brought every type of celebrity into our lives, like John Calvert, best known for his portrayal of the debonair detective in *The Falcon* movies. It was a crazy time and I never knew who I was going to meet.

Pancho Barnes

By far, one of the most interesting of these celebrities was Pancho Barnes. Pancho was an expert pilot whose resume included the founding of the first stunt pilots' union and breaking Amelia Earhart's air speed record. As a young boy, the most interesting thing to me was her ranch. My father and Pancho loved each other for, among other things, their shared passion for flying. Dad was only an amateur, but she was an ace. In addition to her flying exploits, Pancho was also a trick rider, a skill her and Dad shared. That was a great part of their bond.

Pancho frequently had rodeos at her ranch which also featured celebrities like John Calvert who, in addition to acting, was an accomplished magician. One of the biggest stars was Lassie, and my father always accommodated Pancho with a performance.

The ranch was very popular and attracted many pilots from nearby Edwards Air Force Base. It was a great place to relax and have fun and it doubled as a restaurant and bar. Chuck Yeager was a frequent visitor, as was one of the most reclusive men of that era, Howard Hughes. New pilots from Edwards, upon their first visit to Pancho's ranch, were treated to the traditional initiation of getting thrown into the pool while still wearing their clothes. Because of the respect Pancho had for my father, he was never exposed to this ritual. Visits to that ranch were some of my favorite childhood memories.

Emmett Kelly

One time when the circus was in town, my father took me for a ride to show me where it was setting up. We climbed out of the car and found ourselves on a big empty lot. Roustabouts were just setting up the tents. Although opening day was a week away, my dad seemed to have something else in mind as we approached one of the men working on the lot. At the time, I wasn't as impressed as I should have been. The stranger wasn't in costume so the impact of who he was had been lost on me. As Dad introduced us, the man said to me, "Your father helped me get my career started. He trained my little dog to do tricks. The dog passed away, but by then my career was established and I never got another dog." It wasn't until we were leaving that my father told me I had just met the greatest circus clown who ever lived, Emmett Kelly.

Jesse Owens

We were doing an appearance with Lassie in the Canton Football Hall of Fame when my father said, "I want you to come here and shake the hand of the man Hitler wouldn't." I didn't have a clue who he was talking about. That's the way I was introduced to Jesse Owens. I was in my twenties and certainly had heard of Jesse Owens, but when I met him he was probably in his sixties, which seemed old to me. He was bald and, to my surprise, was smoking a cigarette. A former Olympic champion who smoked didn't make sense to me. My father said, "Shake hands with Jesse Owens." Maybe it was because of my youth, but I blurted out, "You smoke?"

"Yes."

"Did you smoke when you were running track?"

"No, I didn't start smoking until I was thirty-six."

Obviously his cigarette had my full attention. "You were a track and field Olympic champion. Why did you start smoking?" He explained, "When I was training, I always wanted to smoke. Everyone was doing it, and it looked like fun. After I was done with my athletic career, I started to smoke." Jesse Owens was a really decent guy who made a terrific ambassador for America at the 1936 Olympics. Sadly, he died in 1980, shortly before his sixty-seventh birthday.

Carl Switzer

While training Petey, the pit bull in the *Our Gang* comedies, my father and Carl "Alfalfa" Switzer became friends. Dad worked on some of the *Our Gang* episodes, although a number of others trained Petey. Dad couldn't take full credit for him, but Petey was his introduction to Carl.

In the early 1950s, Switzer brought Audie Murphy to our house to get some hounds since they were going hunting. Dad had the connections to get all sorts of dogs that he might need for a movie and was able to get them the kind of dogs they wanted. I was very young at the time, probably nine or ten. Alfalfa came to our house and I recognized him immediately.

I was not familiar with the friend he brought along. Years later, when I was a teenager, I went to the premiere of *To Hell and Back* (1955) and Audie was there in his full uniform covered in medals. I finally realized who Alfalfa brought to our home that day. It was Audie Murphy, winner of the Medal of Honor and the most decorated soldier in World War II.

Stubb

In the late 1940's we had a dog named Stubb. He had a peculiar physical attribute that was a bit embarrassing. Besides having a stubby tail, he had an unusually large rectum. He was hired for a photoshoot for an RCA promotion in which he filled the role of the dog listening to the phonograph in the "He Hears His Master's Voice" logo. Luckily he was sitting down.

Karl Miller's dog, Scruffy, the canine star in *The Ghost and Mrs. Muir*, had a similar rectum problem. I was working on a remake of *The Thin Man* and Army Archerd, the famous Hollywood columnist, happened to be visiting the set that day. I was determined not to let Archerd see how I prepared Scruffy for his scenes. Karl, Scruffy's owner, was well aware of his peculiar attribute. There was no way it would play well on camera if Scruffy was filmed from behind while he was walking away.

Karl came up with a great idea. He gave me a powder puff and some powder and told me to use this on Scruffy's butt before each shot. Miraculously, these treatments hid Scruffy's problem from view. At least it wasn't nearly as evident. We could not afford for Scruffy's butt to be stealing scenes or evoking laughter during a serious moment.

One of my father's cardinal rules was to never show the public anything embarrassing regarding the dogs. Always following those rules, I went behind the set to prep Scruffy before he went in front of the camera. This way no one could see me, or so I thought. Actors often study their lines behind the set, close to where they will be needed when their scenes come up. I happened to be powdering Scruffy, when Craig Stevens, the star of the show, came in. He had a quizzical look on his face. Obviously, he had never seen a dog getting his butt powdered before and said, "What are you doing? Does that relax him?" I replied, "No. It relaxes me." He never responded and, with an odd look on his face, accepted my answer and walked away.

Richard Kiel

Richard Kiel was a giant, measuring over seven feet tall, and weighing 335 pounds. I first met Richard long before he threatened James Bond with that mouthful of maniacal metallic teeth. It was 1963, and we were doing a production called *Lassie's Great Adventure,* the first show I worked on after I was hired.

My father knew Richard as a bouncer at his favorite bar, The Rag Doll. Interestingly enough, one of the earlier bouncers at The Rag Doll was Clint Walker, who would one day ride tall in the saddle as the star of the TV Western, *Cheyenne.*

Richard Kiel was also a part-time actor. He frequently asked my father, "Is there anything you can do for me?" *Lassie's Great Adventure* had a great character, a Native American who could neither hear nor speak. Dad told Richard he was just the man for that role. He auditioned and got the part.

In one scene of the movie, Richard was riding a horse. He was so huge that his feet could actually touch the ground. The script called for Richard to have a hawk on his shoulder. The hawk was so intimidating that he spooked the horse. The animal started to buck, as horses tend to do when they are frightened. Richard was so big that he was able to step down and let the horse run out from under him.

One night, after a day of shooting, several of us found our way to a little bar called The Wagon Wheel. We were on location in a small lumberjack town called Sonora, which boasted two bars, the other was The Sonora Inn. As soon as we entered The Wagon Wheel, about six lumberjacks came up to us and asked if we were with the Hollywood crew that was in town. We nodded, since it seemed pretty obvious that we weren't local lumberjacks.

Acting as tough as they could, these hefty guys told us we had better leave the bar while we still could. My friend and I opted for discretion rather than valor and went back to The Sonora Inn. The bar was empty except for Richard Kiel drinking alone. Richard asked us if there was anything interesting going on in this little one-horse town. We told him we were accosted by the lumberjacks over at The Wagon Wheel. "Where is this bar?" Richard asked. I said, "I know you're a big man but there are five or six of them. I don't think it's a good idea to go there." At this point, Richard was thinking more like a professional bouncer than an actor, and said, "I don't care. I'm going over there." We chimed in, "If you're going, we may as well go with you."

The bar at The Wagon Wheel wrapped around the room and went all the way down along the wall. At the far end from the door, the lumberjacks were playing shuffleboard. We found a place at the bar near the door, away from them. Richard sank down behind the bar. It didn't take long for one of the tough guys to notice us. He yelled, "I told you guys to get out of here." He had a beer bottle in his hand as if he was going to break it over my head. That was the moment Richard Kiel decided to stand up, displaying his awesome physical presence. He grabbed the guy by the front of his shirt and actually lifted him into the air. Then the voice of a real giant rumbled through the bar and roared, "See this fist? I can knock your head clean off. I know there are a lot of you. See that guy behind you? After I'm done with you, I will knock him right through the woodwork."

That was a pretty exciting thing to see. Immediately, the atmosphere changed and the lumberjacks welcomed us into their bar. They would not allow us to pay for our drinks, and all the women wanted to dance with Richard. They were especially captivated when he swept them off the ground, with their feet dangling in the air. In the 1960s, there was a popular dance called the Limbo in which the participants were challenged to walk under a pole that was lowered with every pass. Surprisingly, Richard, by far the largest person in the room, was the best that night.

The lumberjacks were also enjoying themselves, shouting, "We have Paul Bunyan here!" They couldn't believe it and neither could we. That night at The Wagon Wheel, we left reality behind and the evening unfolded just like in a Hollywood movie scene.

The next day we had to shoot a scene where a runaway hot air balloon, carrying Jon Provost and Lassie, landed in a tree. Lassie and Jon were in the balloon while I, along with Murphy, the special effects man, were high in the air in an apparatus called a boom. We had a special harness on Lassie, played in this movie by Spook. The harness allowed Jon to lower the dog from the basket. From the camera's perspective, it looked like Jon was lowering Lassie with a rope looped around the limb of the tree. The shot ended with Timmy and Lassie safe on the ground and the director told the cast and crew to break for lunch. It happened to be Thanksgiving Day and a very special lunch awaited us. Everybody immediately rushed off to the catering trucks. There was only one problem. In their rush to be first in line for turkey and all the trimmings, everyone had forgotten about Murphy and me in the boom. We were stranded high off the ground.

By the time we realized that we had been forgotten, no one was within yelling distance. Much later, someone back on the main set noticed that we were missing. A ladder truck finally arrived back at the tree. By then, lunch was over and the caterers were cleaning up. All Murphy and I could salvage were a few black olives. Incidentally, the director who left us stranded for hours without ever noticing we were missing, was none other than William Beaudine Sr.

Clint Walker

The Rag Doll bar was one of my father's favorite places to relax and have a drink. He was there so often that he would sometimes sleep there. Long before Richard Kiel worked there as a bouncer, Clint Walker was charged with keeping the peace on the premises. During his tenure, Walker had to confront a number of people. In fact, he bounced my father out of there on one occasion.

Walker had just thrown out a rowdy customer when my dad walked in the back door, minding his own business. Walker thought he was the same person who just got thrown out, trying to sneak back in. Walker was having none of it. He grabbed my father and lifted him in the air, his arms locked firmly around my dad's ribs. Clint didn't know the magnitude of his own strength. His firm grip broke my father's ribs. At that point, he could have been fired, and with the loss of his steady Rag Doll income, he might have had to abandon his Hollywood dream. My father didn't do anything to get him fired. He surely could have because he was a frequent customer. Not only did he own Lassie, but he also spent a good deal of time and money there. He also entertained some very important people who held their kids' birthday parties at The Rag Doll, because they knew Lassie would show up as a big surprise for their children.

My father needed some payback, but nothing as drastic as getting Walker fired. As an aspiring actor, a cash settlement was not something Clint Walker could afford. While my father did many good things for the world, he was far from ever reaching sainthood. He seemed equally at home with studio tycoons as he did with characters who could best be described as thugs. Bob Brennan fell into the latter category. He enjoyed a good brawl, probably because he was a retired prizefighter. He no doubt missed the glory days in the ring. Bob Brennan became the instrument of my father's revenge on Clint Walker.

One night, Brennan and Walker came face-to-face in back of The Rag Doll. Brennan threw a punch that knocked Walker out cold. Then he reported back to my father, "I knocked him out and shoved him into a trash can, Rudd, but he was too big. He didn't fit in that can." Clint Walker may have suffered a few bruises for breaking my father's ribs, but Dad stopped short of ending his livelihood and potentially his future Hollywood career. Clint went on to fit into some pretty big cowboy boots as Cheyenne Bodie on the TV series, *Cheyenne*, and combat boots in the movie, *The Dirty Dozen* (1967).

Bob Hope

One night, we were sitting at home and my dad was watching television. The phone rang and he gave us orders to tell the caller that he was not at home. Dad didn't like to be bothered when he was watching TV, especially on Sunday nights. "Tell them I'm in bed. Tell them anything. Tell them I'm not at home." My mother said, "I think you should take this call."

"Who is it?"

"Bob Hope."

"The real Bob Hope?"

"Yes, the real Bob Hope."

It turned out that Bob Hope and one of his writers were passing time at his home, brainstorming some new skit ideas for *The Bob Hope Show*. As they talked, Lassie came to mind and they started formulating a storyline in which Lassie would appear on his show in a skit that spoofed the popular program, *This Is Your Life*. My father was glad he took the call. Lassie appeared on Bob Hope's TV show and both men became good friends.

Years later, my dad and I were doing another show for Bob Hope after Dad had just celebrated his birthday. Jack Wrather presented Dad with a beautiful belt buckle and a thousand-dollar bill. He was really proud of this bill and he showed it to Bob Hope and said, "Look what I have in my wallet." Bob, with his great sense of humor and quick thinking noticed that Red Skelton just entered the studio. He called him over and said, "Red, show Rudd what you have in your wallet." Skelton pulled out his wallet. In it was a hundred-thousand dollars in ten-thousand dollar bills. After Skelton walked away, the conversation turned serious. Dad asked, "Why does he have that much money in his wallet?" Bob Hope answered, "He lived through the Depression and he never forgot the experience. Now he keeps that money in his wallet in case everything collapses again and he needs a room or something to eat." Behind the public image of a happy-go-lucky Red Skelton was a person constantly aware of the financial uncertainty of his past.

Johnny Carson

Johnny Carson was a lot like Bob Hope. His mind worked very quickly. That's why he was able to ad lib so well. The first time I was introduced to Johnny Carson was when my father made an appearance on *The Tonight Show* to promote Recipe dog food. Lassie, at the time, was Hey Hey. Before the show, I warned my father not to let him start barking because he'd never stop. Once Hey Hey got into the barking mode he wouldn't do anything else. My father ignored my advice and, while he was interviewed by Carson, he had the dog bark. After that, Hey Hey would not stop barking. Eventually Carson could no longer ignore it and asked my father, "Why is that dog barking?" On *The Tonight Show,* where a fast quip was worth its weight in gold, my father responded, "He wants more money."

Arthur Treacher

Hey Hey was one crazy dog. He enjoyed playing the role of Lassie. He was a ham. During an appearance on *The Merv Griffin Show*, the producers wanted Hey Hey to jump into my arms. Arthur Treacher sat on a chair off to the side. Dad was holding the dog on one end and I was standing between a table and Arthur Treacher. My father got Hey Hey excited and the huge collie took off at an incredible speed, like a missile. He shot high into the air and was obviously going to leap well beyond where I was standing. I quickly moved back to catch him and the momentum almost knocked me over. I did manage to bend down, but when I did, we were almost in a horrified Arthur Treacher's lap. At that point, Hey Hey's face was up against Treacher's and the excited collie gave him a kiss. It was a great performance for the studio audience and the cameras. I'm not sure Arthur Treacher would agree.

Vincent Price

The Weatherwax ranch was a popular destination for many celebrities who wanted a few personal moments with America's most beloved collie. As Dad and I were conducting a training session, I saw a car coming down the road. Following it was a vehicle that looked like a catering truck. Dad noticed the puzzled look on my face and said, "Yeah, I forgot to tell you that Vincent Price is coming up. He has a little girl who wants to meet Lassie." I responded, "I thought we were training today." Dad said, "We are, but this won't take long. We'll have Lassie do a few things and he will just take a few pictures. Then we'll get back to training."

The truck pulled up and it carried gourmet food, including stuffed pheasants and fine wine. It was Vincent Price's way of reciprocating the favor. We all had a great lunch that day. The truck contained a dining area and all the facilities we needed. Vincent Price was so tall that he had to duck when he went in and out of the truck.

Louis Armstrong

I always enjoyed Louis Armstrong's music, especially "Hello, Dolly." That man was the greatest trumpet player that ever lived and, thanks to Lassie, I met him one night in San Francisco when we were doing a publicity appearance. Lassie's routine always required a late night walk and an early morning stroll. Fewer people were out and about at those times and Dad definitely did not want anyone to see Lassie taking care of his natural business. As we entered the hotel lobby after the walk, I noticed a distinguished looking gentleman and his wife walking ahead of us. He happened to turn around and looked at the collie. "Is that Lassie?" he asked. I said, "Yes." "May I pet him?," he asked. While I assured him he could pet the dog, I was dealing with my own celebrity moment. That was definitely Louis Armstrong and now it was my turn to make a request. "May I shake your hand? I love your music and I have all of it in my collection." We shook hands and spoke briefly. Then his wife reminded him that it was time to go to bed. Louis Armstrong was another wonderful person I will never forget.

George Foreman

I was coming in from lunch when we were working on *The New Lassie* TV show at Universal Studios. There was a Mexican restaurant right across the street. We just finished lunch and were on our way back to the studio.

I noticed a large man walking down the sidewalk with what appeared to be a bodyguard. I recognized him instantly as boxing great George Foreman. Ever since I could remember, I had followed his career and admired him. I pulled the car over, jumped out, and ran over to him. "Are you George Foreman?," I asked. He said, "Yes." I quickly said to him, "I'm a fan of yours. I've followed your career, and especially remember the time at the Olympics when you held up a little flag. I'm not one to collect autographs, but I sure would like to have yours." He asked if I had anything to write on. The car was right there so I grabbed the script we were working on that day. I told him that was all I really had so he signed the script. I thanked him and started to walk away. Just then, he called me back and said, "Wait a minute. That script said Lassie. Do you have anything to do with Lassie?" I told him that my father and I owned all the Lassies. He said, "Well, come back here. I want to shake your hand." What a powerful handshake that was.

These were all fascinating people, whose careers enriched my life and the lives of many Americans. My father's work brought him in contact with giants who actually made history and he recognized how fortunate he was to have those opportunities. I am forever grateful to him for recognizing the value of sharing those experiences.

15

The Duke of Hollywood

MY FATHER AND I not only got to know some of the most interesting people, but also shared some of the same experiences in our career paths. One of the most contentious was working with the Duke himself, John Wayne. He stood as tall in the eyes of American moviegoers as he did in the saddle, viewed by many as a true hero.

Wayne was cast in a Western called *Hondo* (1953), for Warner Brothers. The director was John Farrow. Farrow had a solid list of directing credits at the time. My father worked on two movies with him. One was *Hondo* and the other was *A Bullet Is Waiting* (1954), starring Rory Calhoun and Jean Simmons. Dad said that John Farrow was very difficult to work with on the set of *Hondo*. There was a marked change the following year, when he was working on *A Bullet Is Waiting*. He noticed that John Farrow was much easier to work with. When my father asked him about this, Farrow replied that he started to see himself in John Wayne and he didn't like what he saw.

Hollywood insiders regarded John Wayne as a man who was very difficult to work with. They claimed that Wayne liked to keep the crew intimidated and they spoke of working in constant fear of losing their jobs. I can only guess that John Wayne thought he could get better work out of them that way.

Back in the day when Westerns ruled the movie screens, dogs would frequently show up as faithful companions. Whenever a dog was written into a script, John Wayne would do his best to disrupt the trainers on the very first day. If he could get them fired early in the production, the dog would be written out of the script and he wouldn't have to deal with them. The Duke liked to mention that W. C. Fields preached that it was never a good thing to work with dogs or kids. They made mistakes and held up production. My father worked with W.C. Fields. Fields knew kids and dogs didn't necessarily hold up production. He didn't want anyone taking the spotlight from him.

My father was hired to provide the dog in the movie *Hondo* (1953) starring John Wayne. The movie was made in Camargo, Mexico, at the same time they were filming the opening scenes for the new *Lassie* series. Dad felt that he should have been there for the *Lassie* show, but the contract for *Hondo* had already been signed. Frank Inn had to handle the home front.

My father drove to Mexico in his DeSoto with two dogs, Pal and Red Wool. Pal, although he carried the same name, was not the original Lassie. This dog, Pal, was purchased from a man named Red Morton and had been used as a double for the first TV Lassie because he was very physical. He was shorter and stockier than Lassie and could be used for some of the more demanding parts such as running over hills or jumping. This allowed them to continue working rather than having to wait for Lassie to stop panting and drooling. The other dog, Red Wool, was borrowed from Frank Weatherwax. Although Pal would be the only dog used in the movie, the production company insisted on an additional dog as a backup and Red Wool filled that role.

It did not take long for my father to experience the pressure that was an intricate part of working with John Wayne. The first thing Wayne did was to try to get my father fired. What John Wayne did was attempt to foul up the trainer by complaining that the dog was going to hold up production. Wayne tried to pull this same stunt on my father in *Hondo*.

The very first day of production, Dad and the dog were off to the side waiting until they were needed. When the crew called for him, he started to run back to the set. He always had a pack of Lucky Strikes in his shirt pocket. As he ran, he held his hand over the left pocket to prevent the cigarettes from falling out. John Wayne watched the whole thing. Even though he knew better, he shouted, "Oh, we can't use this man. Look. He's gonna have a heart attack," implying he was clenching his chest in pain.

As the days passed, Dad became more and more concerned about the events unfolding at home. With the new TV series foremost on his mind, Dad decided to fire himself and leave the dogs. He was told that no one quits. When Dad went to get in his car to leave, he found his tires slashed and could not get new ones until the movie was complete. Stuck in Camargo, he made the best of the situation finding common interests with Wayne in drinking, smoking, and playing poker.

Dad and Duke Wayne got in a card game one night. Dad was beating Wayne for a while but Wayne was able to stay in the game using the production company's petty money. Petty money on this picture was probably $40,000, and so he simply had more money. Wayne was able to continue playing until fortune turned his way. When Dad eventually ran out of money, he pulled a bluff that was never used in any poker game. To stay in the game, he put up his most valuable asset, Lassie. At least that's what my father led the Duke to believe. Wayne was under the impression that the collie used in the movie was actually the same one who played Lassie. In reality, the real Lassie was in Washington with Frank Inn filming the opening scenes of the show.

Dad lost and Duke Wayne took possession of what he thought was a great American icon. What he won, in fact, was a replica. He was so proud of this conquest that he bragged about it for years after. My father, being a master grifter, never let Wayne in on his little bait-and-switch. That would not be the end of the story.

John Wayne had a stunt double, Chuck Roberson, who also had a small part in the movie. There was a scene in which Roberson, standing in for Wayne, was riding his horse while being chased by the bad guys. The scene was on a very steep hill and, because it was very difficult to prepare, the stuntmen were demanding more money. The local townspeople who were playing the bad guys were amused by this because navigating those hills on horseback was part of their daily lives. The scene called for Wayne, or in this case his stunt double, to get away from the villains and, while in a full gallop, pick up his dog who was waiting for him in the field.

To facilitate the stunt, my father prepared a harness for Pal to make it easier for Roberson to pick him up. Wayne watched with amusement. He didn't believe my father could get the dog to stand still with all those horses stampeding toward him. He proposed another wager that would give my father a chance to win back the dog who he thought was Lassie. If the dog stayed put for the scene, my father got him back. If he ran, John Wayne keeps Lassie. Wayne could never imagine how well my father knew his dogs. Dad knew Pal was a good, sturdy, and steady dog. He stood there like a statue waiting to be picked up. The scene was a success and Dad had his dog back.

John Wayne was not my father's only headache in Camargo, Mexico. Red Wool, the dog my father brought down as a backup, escaped one night and decided to explore the Mexican countryside. Someone left a door open by accident. Eventually some locals caught up with the canine tourist with the furry tail but refused to return him to the production company. Incredibly, they decided to hold him for ransom. They assumed he was the animal star of the movie and the filming could not continue without him. The production people ignored the ransom demands. After all, Red Wool was only the stand-by dog. Pal was doing all of the work in front of the cameras. My father had a much different view of the matter. He always took care of his dogs. He wanted him back unharmed before he left Mexico. Dad paid the ransom and brought Red Wool home, safe and sound.

Eighteen years later, in 1971, my career and that of my father crossed paths, as seemed to happen often. A new Wayne extravaganza was in the works and the production manager for the movie came to our ranch. Having some experience with Dad and his dogs in *Hondo,* it was natural that they would consider him for this movie. They were looking for a dog that would attack and be able to run with horses without hesitation. At the time, my father was doing the *Lassie* show and had no interest in returning to Mexico for another round of slashed tires. I was not in business for myself at the time, but he referred them to me. I had a dog, Laddie, who was a great attack dog. His eyes would light up at the chance to go at someone. I also had another dog named Silver, who was great at running with horses. Between the two, the producers found a great combination for the movie that would become *Big Jake* (1971).

I had never done a movie before and my father was concerned that my first movie experience would be with John Wayne. He warned me that Wayne was the most difficult person he ever worked with and that he could sour me on the movie business. I didn't heed his warning and headed for Durango, Mexico with Laddie and Silver. I just turned thirty when I did *Big Jake*. I had worked a lot of shows, but as my father's assistant. There I was, doing my first movie with one of the silver screen's biggest stars. It was just a bit overwhelming.

Big Jake had a great cast. John Wayne was the main star, supported by the beautiful Maureen O'Hara. Other cast members included the Duke's two sons, Ethan and Patrick. Rounding out the cast were Richard Boone, Bruce Cabot, Jim Davis, John Agar, and Harry Carey Jr. John Wayne's son, Michael, was the producer.

John Wayne's character owned a rough collie named Dog. Throughout his vast body of film work, Wayne managed to do without dogs in co-starring roles in all but two of his movies, *Hondo* and *Big Jake*. Both movies featured Weatherwax dogs. As for the rest, you might catch a glimpse of a dog running across a street as the stagecoach arrives, nothing more.

The Duke was in his usual form and the production company soothed the roiled waters by paying people extra money to work with him. It didn't take long for me to discover why Dad felt the way he did about the legendary John Wayne. When John Wayne came on the set, we hadn't started shooting the movie yet. I didn't recognize him at first because he wasn't wearing his toupee. He was facing sideways, shirtless, and throwing a football. I noticed the scar from his cancer surgery and I heard his voice. That's when it dawned on me. This must be John Wayne.

Before long, the Duke came up to me and we were introduced. His first words to me were, "I won Lassie from your father in a card game, but I gave the dog back because I felt sorry for your Dad." That's when I made my first mistake. I corrected him and said, "No, you didn't win Lassie, because at the time Lassie was shooting a pilot for the TV series. What you won was a stand-in." There was silence, the kind that makes your soul wither. Wayne just stared at me and I knew it wasn't the start of a beautiful friendship.

It didn't take long for that trouble to bubble up on the set. In one scene, Wayne was scripted to walk into a bar with his friend. The dog was supposed to see him enter, follow, and sit next to him. I had the scene set up with a stand-in and the dog knew exactly what he had to do. Then Wayne came in and took over for the stand-in. He tugged at the dog who then became confused. I asked, "What are you doing?"

"How the hell are you going to get the dog to come in?"

"I already have that worked out. He knows exactly where to go."

"Well, I think you're in the wrong spot."

"Well, I think I'm in the right spot."

"Oh, you're a know-it-all."

"Well, I don't know everything, but I know what I'm doing here, Mr. Wayne."

"You don't call me Mr. Wayne."

"Okay, John."

"You don't call me John, either. I am the Duke!"

By now, the crew was getting a bit nervous. The confrontation had gone on long enough. He blew his lines in that scene seventeen times. A veteran actor like him does not require that many takes to get a scene right. He did that deliberately in the hopes that the dog would eventually screw up. It just didn't happen. The only one screwing up on purpose was John Wayne. It was a complicated scene for the dog because he had to wander in and sit down while the actors talked. When they were finished with their dialogue, the dog had to follow Wayne upstairs. Again, the dog performed beautifully.

Ironically, the incident that caused me to want to quit didn't originate with anything John Wayne threw at me. It was the director, George Sherman, who pulled the pin on my grenade. If there was one thing that could make that grenade go off, it was insulting one of my dogs. If Bill Beaudine Sr. calling Lassie a meat hound got under my father's skin, George Sherman's remark drilled right through to my bones.

As we were about to shoot a scene, Sherman began to walk up a hill and barked "get the mother#*!%," referring to my dog. I shot up that hill after him like a heat-seeking missile and confronted him. I exploded, "If you ever call my dog that name again I will beat your brains out!" Sherman then did a really bizarre thing. He stiffened up, turned sideways, stood like a soldier at attention, and said, "OK, I get it." Just then, I noticed that John Wayne had joined us and asked, "What's going on here?" I was still in attack mode and barked, "Nothing I can't handle!" and walked back down the hill.

I didn't know if Sherman "got it" but I had it. I told the production manager that I was quitting the project. I would leave the dogs and send another trainer. I didn't have any tires to slash like my father and I packed to head home. There was one problem. The production manager had my visa and he wasn't giving it back. There I was, just like my father eighteen years earlier, stranded in Mexico. Another Weatherwax was taken hostage by a John Wayne production.

John Wayne never called my dog names, but he was definitely not dog's best friend. As the movie progressed, John's son Michael, the producer, noticed that the dogs were not paying attention to his father's character like a real pet would. He wanted me to get the dog to focus more on Wayne. I suggested that the only way to do that was to have his father feed the dog. I always carried a small bag of food. If Wayne would feed the dog, it would help build a bond. That did not go well with Wayne. Michael told his father the plan and I brought the bag of food over to him. "So now you want me to do your job? Are you gonna give me half your pay too?," Wayne asked, and threw the bag of food to the ground. I gathered up the food, put it back in the bag, and the plan was abandoned.

To accomplish the bonding, I came up with another idea. When Wayne was sitting on his horse, I'd reach over the horse's neck with the food so the dog would think it was the rider feeding him. As soon as Wayne noticed what I was doing, he turned his horse into me to try to knock me over. It was vintage Wayne, never wanting the crew to feel comfortable.

John Wayne was a lot like the characters he played in the movies. I asked his son Michael why his father was still acting. He didn't seem to enjoy it anymore. Michael told me that his father lost a lot of money making *The Alamo* (1960) and he was trying to recoup some of his losses. Like all of us, the Duke was dealing with some of life's most distracting and discouraging issues, money and health. Problems such as these can make any of us most unpleasant to deal with. His loyal crew members seemed to understand this. They were always complaining about working with Wayne. I remarked to one of them, "I bet you won't ever do a movie for him again." The guy quickly responded, "Oh no, I work for him all the time. We just get extra pay." They called it John Wayne pay. That's how he kept his crew one production after another. Extra cash can soothe a lot of wounds inflicted on the set.

If anyone understood the Duke on that movie set, it had to be his kids. His youngest boy, Ethan, was about nine years old at the time we were shooting *Big Jake*. He drove around the set on a little motor scooter and he loved to hang out with me and the dog. One day, Ethan came riding over to visit and the production people must have told his father that the sound of the scooter ruined a shot. The next thing I saw was this huge cowboy, riding hell-bent for leather toward us on horseback.

The tall rider reigned in near Ethan and in that voice and drawl known throughout the world he said, "You do that one more time and I'm going to throw you and that scooter over the cliff." Like any good gunslinger, the Duke spit a wad of tobacco near his son. Then he wheeled the horse around and rode off. I looked at Ethan and he was smiling. That was his dad, whom he loved and admired. Everyone else was afraid of John Wayne but Ethan didn't bat an eye. He kept up his conversation with me but made sure not to drive back on the motorbike while cameras were rolling. The whole incident seemed right out of a movie. With John Wayne, his life mimicked the movies.

My father's fear that shooting a movie with John Wayne would ruin me never materialized. Working on *Big Jake* just made me tougher. Anytime I ran into a difficult director or producer, I used to think, *Hell, I worked with John Wayne. You don't intimidate me.*

There was one attribute my father and I did share with The Duke. He was a perfectionist and took great pride in the work he did. I recall one day when a crew member made a major mistake by stating, "Well, I don't know why everybody's worried. It's just another movie." Wayne overheard him, turned around and bellowed, "What do you mean this is just another movie?" The tirade continued for quite some time until the man wished he could shrink so tiny as to be invisible.

John Wayne with cast and crew on the set of *Big Jake* (1971)

I feel the same way as John Wayne did about our work. I once had a trainer work for me who said, "I don't know why you worry about the shot, Bob. It's just another movie." I blew up just like the Duke did. You can't think of a production in that way. If my father looked at *Lassie Come Home* as if it were just another movie, it would be among the ranks of forgotten films today. My father did all his movies to perfection. A lot of people lost good opportunities in Hollywood because of a cavalier attitude toward their work. John Wayne fully understood the implications

133

of giving a production less than the very best effort. Like Dad and me, the Duke found that intolerable. In that regard, the Weatherwax family, along with John Wayne, have always been a breed apart.

Professional opinions and personal opinions do not always coincide. It was that way with John Wayne. I admire the man and the work he did. He was the superstar of his era and I will be the first to acknowledge the huge contribution he made to the motion picture industry. John Wayne was a giant in Hollywood and I am proud to this day to boast that I had the privilege of working with him. He was truly the Duke of Hollywood.

16

The Making of a Star

THE WORKING SPAN of a Lassie was about eight years and it took roughly two of those years to train the collie. During this time, we were not only teaching response to commands, but also shaping personalities. Around the age of six, we would start planning for his successor and breed him. None of the Lassies were neutered and every litter was sired by the prior Lassie, except one. Pal's line ended with the death of his grandson, Laddie. All of the subsequent Weatherwax Lassies were descended from the original TV Lassie, that wild-child canine who chomped on Frank Inn's expensive suit.

People don't realize that there have been many different Lassies, each with his own personality. Every time my father trained a new Lassie he used different techniques. In this way he was able to duplicate the previous Lassie so that no one realized it was a new dog. We never used a double except occasionally in a distant shot. Up close, it was always just one dog, and that was Lassie.

Dad's work with the dogs was truly amazing. No matter what type of personality traits the animal possessed, Dad created and preserved the image of Lassie each and every time. It didn't matter whether they were easily frightened, nervous, or aggressive, they were all trained to become professional canine stars. The proof is preserved in the movies we made and the television shows we filmed. What set him apart, and what I see as the core of the Weatherwax story is that, like a superior athlete, my father made something very complex look very simple. He did things with dogs that have never been done before, or since. Every twitch of the ear, each subtle turn of the head, and any movement of the tail was choreographed by Dad. When the dogs displayed mood changes, they were acting. He was an artist and his canvas was a collie. Things didn't always go as planned. Lassie III, also known as Baby, was one of my father's favorite Lassies. We had planned to work him another two years but he developed cancer when he was only six years old. This devastated my father. He loved each of his dogs but had a special affection for this one. More than losing a star dog, Dad was losing a cherished friend. My father did everything to save him. When Baby lost his hair, Dad had Max Factor make hairpieces to cover his bald patches. Although my father had to continue working, he wanted to spend as much time as possible with Baby.

Dad used to take the retired Lassies to work at times because they would cry when the current Lassie went in the car instead of them. Following that practice, he took Baby with him to the set most days, and put him on a blanket where he could watch the activity. Baby would sit up and seemed to enjoy what he could, until he lost his battle. His son, Lassie IV, nicknamed Mire, was only eleven months old at the time. This was much too young to start working him as a Lassie, but we had no choice. As in human families, the illness of one generation affects generations that follow. Such was the case with Baby's untimely death. Pressing Mire into service at such an early age was extremely hard on him and, as a result, he had to be retired early.

Although we sometimes had nicknames for our dogs, like Spook or Baby, in public Dad always called the dog Lassie. Whether at home, public appearances, or printed on first-class plane tickets, the name was Lassie. Nicknames were just a convenient means of reference. When we called them, or when someone else called them, the name used was Lassie.

All the dogs destined to become Lassie were called Laddie at first. When we replaced the reigning collie, the successor became Lassie. My mother had a habit that always upset my father when it came to Pal. After he made the MGM movies, he became Lassie. Mom still called him Pal. Dad would object, "Don't call him Pal, he's Lassie." Mom always overruled his objection with, "We'll worry about that with the next one. To me, he's Pal." After Pal, Mom relented. She had a little routine with the dog that was the first Lassie on television. She would say to him, "Who's got the money? Who writes the checks?" He'd get up, run over to the desk where she worked, and look at her. It was funny to watch.

Dad was often asked which dog was the best Lassie. Without fail he would answer, "The dog I have now." Although Pal was probably his greatest, Dad was of the opinion that the present Lassie was his best. At every point in his life he looked forward, never dwelling in the past. In fact, he would never watch the old Lassie movies. He couldn't bring himself to watch the dogs he had lost. It was much too heart-wrenching for him.

Over the years, the Lassie legacy intertwined with that of the name Weatherwax. The Weatherwax collies became the movie icons without relying on any particular human co-star. No actor made Lassie. He was always the star. The Lassie productions went through numerous cast changes and employed different storylines, but the only constant throughout Lassie's success was the Weatherwax genius.

Baby

These skills were passed from father to son, as it was with my grandfather to my father, again repeating the cycle with Dad and me. At the core of the Weatherwax success was a relentless work ethic. There is a story my father told me when I was a young man starting out in the business. During a particularly frustrating training session, I gave up and decided to cut it short. My dad stopped me and insisted, "You can't finish like that. If you do, the dog has won." He then told me a story that gives a fascinating insight into the mindset of a Weatherwax.

One day, Dad took one of his father's horses and thought he would show off and make him jump over a fence. Instead, the horse balked and threw him. Walter came out and said to Dad, "Do you see what you did? You can't leave him like that. Now I have to finish what you started." Then Walter got on the horse and tried to make him jump over the fence. The horse decided to go sideways into the fence. He did this about three times until Walter finally got him to jump. He then got off the horse, went up to my father and said, "Now, you have to cut my boot off." He had fractured his foot one of the times the horse crashed into the fence. Despite great pain, Walter would not give up, even with a broken foot. He knew the horse would have been spoiled for any further training because of my father. That was the kind of tough characters the Weatherwax men were. They had a work ethic which stayed with my father and was passed down to me.

These lessons were vital to the success of the Weatherwax dogs. Other trained dogs just had to perform a function. No one cares about the dog's disposition, just as long as he does his job. Our dogs had to act. We had to control the dogs' ears, the wagging of their tails, their speed, and how high their head was. All these things convey the emotion and reaction called for by the scene. Sometimes those emotions would have to change in the middle of a scene.

Imagine the intricacies of training dogs for the film industry. They have to know more than eighty different commands and do them at different speeds. In the movie industry, time is money. When the director tells us to do a scene he doesn't know or care how the dog is going to do it, he just wants it done. We had to be prepared to do what the director wanted.

There is a scene in *The Courage of Lassie* (1946) in which Elizabeth Taylor is in bed with the measles. Lassie initially comes in happy to see her then realizes she is sick in bed. One can see his disposition changing. His tail stops wagging, his ears go down, and he starts walking more slowly toward her. His speed changes, he walks over, and puts his head on the bed. Then she tells him, "It's OK Lassie, it's just the measles." With this, he perks up a bit and puts his head on her chest. That one scene involved a multitude of commands and voice inflections. Demanding scenes such as these illustrate why, for a dog to become Lassie, it took years of planning and hard work.

The incredible skill and effort my father put into training all his dogs paid off by producing scenes that were sometimes heartwarming and often spectacular. The goal was always to have the audience believe the dog was thinking for himself. Whether it was tenderly comforting a sick little girl or performing a daring rescue, Weatherwax dogs made it all look natural. That was the uniqueness of my father.

Early in his career, Dad had to work alone since no helper was available. Simple things for human actors, like finding a mark to know where to stand, were much more difficult with a dog. If there were two trainers, they could position themselves on opposite sides of the set. One called the dog and, when he reached his mark, the other stopped him and turned him around. Without a second trainer, this was not possible. Dad solved the problem for the small sum of ten cents.

My father taught each of his dogs to put a foot on a dime. If he wanted the dog to go to the middle of a room and stop at a certain spot, he put a dime there and sent the dog. When the dog saw the dime he put his foot on it, thereby covering it from the view of the audience. The dog was standing in the right place and could be moved using the same technique.

My dad's training also allowed us to do long takes which are continuous scenes without cuts. Doing a scene with a lot of cuts looks a bit choppy and takes away some of the credibility. There was one shot we did in which Lassie rescued horses from a burning barn. To accomplish this, Sam Williamson sat on a hill and released Lassie. Supposedly, Lassie saw the smoke coming from the barn. There were three horses in the barn. I waited at the bottom of the hill near the barn, which had a rope on the door. I directed Lassie to pick up the rope and bring it to me. It appeared that Lassie opened the door. At that moment my father, standing inside the barn, took over and told Lassie to drop the rope and come toward him. Inside, Dad had Lassie nudge the boards that held the horses' gates in place. He hit the first one and the horse ran out. He hit the second one with his nose and the horse kicked up and ran out. The third horse wouldn't go. That horse happened to be wearing a hackamore. My father told Lassie to pick up the rope and I told him to bring it to me far enough out of the barn. It appeared he was pulling the horse out. When he was far enough from the barn, I told him to drop the rope and I then yelled to Sam. Sam called Lassie, which made him appear to be running back up the hill for help. With that, we had a very complicated scene, done without cuts, in one take.

There was one episode in which Lassie was lost in San Francisco. He traveled the city and as soon as he got to the Golden Gate Bridge, he put his feet up to look over the rail. The camera was positioned behind him to capture everything he did. The trainer had to be out of sight but close enough to tell Lassie when to put his feet up. That's where I came in. Sam was afraid of heights and my father was the head trainer. I pulled the short straw. They hung me by a rope under the bridge where Lassie was standing. Originally, they were going to give the job of holding the rope to the special effects man, who was small and elderly. I said, "No, I think we need somebody a little bigger and a little younger." I didn't want to insult the guy but my life was literally hanging on this. We were just at the beginning of the bridge so I didn't have to worry about the water, only the large boulders underneath. We got the shot, and I survived the Golden Gate Bridge.

My father wanted to do a scene where Lassie would jump from the ground to the back of a horse and into my arms. Before I began training dogs, Frank Inn was considered the best at catching Lassie. Later, my father told me that I was even better than Frank. I was stunned since it was nearly impossible to get a compliment out of him, and that one was a big one.

Hey Hey, Lassie V, was the craziest dog we ever had. He was the best candidate for jumping onto a horse, then to me. He would jump anywhere, not caring whether or not he could see me or where he would land. The first time we tried this stunt, Hey Hey broke into a full run. He jumped from the table and jumped on the back of a horse. The dog was in the air but I could see that he wasn't coming towards me. I had to run in the direction from which he was coming and catch him. At that crucial moment, I lost my balance and went to my knees. Fortunately, I didn't get the dog hurt. I took the blow myself by grabbing him and going to my knees. Then we did it a second time. I went down again. Finally, Hey Hey knew where I was. The third time we did the stunt, he jumped high in the air and came right to me. There was still such an impact that I went down into a squat. I was sore for days, but we got the shot.

Waking up with aches and pains became a way of life for me as I was also designated by Dad to be Lassie's protector and bodyguard. Dad made sure I knew that if there was danger on the set, such as wild animals getting loose or an explosive stunt gone wrong, it was my responsibility to call or grab Lassie and get out. I had to do this twice to get Lassie to safety. My father did not want stuntmen working on a scene with Lassie either. He was afraid they wouldn't protect the dog.

Sam Williamson used to do all the stunt work that involved Lassie. When I started working with my father in 1962 I took on that role. Sam was getting older and it was a very physically demanding thing to do. In one such scene I was shooting a rifle and Lassie had to jump from a rock and knock me down. To accomplish this, my father would first have Lassie jump into my arms as we usually did. Then, with that trick on his mind, we had him go back on the rock and tell him to jump to me again, this time while I was holding the rifle. Then as he leaped, I turned my back causing him to knock me down.

In *The Magic of Lassie* (1978) a police officer, acting on information in a wanted poster, tried to capture Lassie. I stunt doubled as the officer. Lassie was on a little boat and leaped at me as if I was going to catch him. Instead, I let him hit me in the chest and knock me down. I should have had better padding for that. I went down on the cement road and was limping for a day.

If there were any wild animals on the set, I had to be sure that Lassie was protected from any danger. Lassie had to work with a lot of species, but we always kept him away from dangerous animals, filming them separately then cutting back and forth so they looked like they were together in the same shot. Some wild animal suppliers didn't have control of their animals and a collie dog could be considered dinner. Regardless of the risk to myself, my job was to get Lassie out of harm's way if necessary. Once we were working with a mountain lion who got loose on the set. I immediately grabbed Lassie and carried him out of the building to the safety of our car. While I was getting Lassie out of danger, the puma was still busy wreaking havoc in the studio. The puma bit our key grip, Big John, on the pants leg. The trainers were pulling the cat by his hind legs but he wasn't letting go. Finally, someone from wardrobe came over with a pair of scissors and cut Big John's pants and let the cat have the fabric. Big John looked funny the rest of the day with just one pant leg, but at least he had his leg.

We also had to watch out for overly aggressive directors. On the *Lassie* series there was an episode in which the script called for a man to ride up to Lassie on a horse. Lassie then had to bark as if to say follow me. My father told the man riding the horse where to stop so he didn't hurt Lassie. Before they shot the scene, Dad noticed the director talking to that same man on the horse. He turned to me and said, "Do you know what that's all about?" I said, "No." Dad said, "He's telling that guy to ride up closer to the dog to get a better shot. You have to watch for these guys. They will do that every time and they will hurt the dog." Before the cameras rolled, my father told the rider to stop where he originally told him. He responded that the director wanted him to do something different. My father warned him that he would never work on the show again if he risked Lassie by doing what that director wanted him to do. We had to be vigilant around certain directors who did not care much about the actors and worried even less about the animals, concerning themselves only with getting that sensational shot at any cost.

Looking Glass was an aircraft that provided an airborne command base in the event all ground command was not operable. I never heard of this before, but we were shooting an episode of *Lassie* in Riverside and Jack Wrather had planes from the Strategic Air Command flown in to support the plot. The storyline featured a diabetic poodle who accidentally boarded Looking Glass and Lassie had to let someone know that the poodle was in trouble. They brought the plane down and saved the poodle.

I asked Jack Wrather how expensive it was to bring those planes here. He said $17,000 each, one way, but the Air Force used it as a recruiting tool. I was given a tour of the aircraft, which was designed to be undetectable by radar. I don't think this is something that you would be able to do today.

We did a similar show in Lompoc, California where many of our ICBM missile silos are located. There we got a tour of the war room and the site's silos. The silos have large concrete slabs protecting them in the event of an attack. To open them to launch a missile, explosives force the slab to push back on rollers. The episode dealt with a duck who made a nest on one of the slabs. Lassie had to let someone know the duck was in danger. After the duck was safe, they actually launched a missile for us. I asked where it was going and was told Australia. There was nothing to worry about because they could put it down in an area the size of a football field and no one in Australia was endangered, since they were made aware of the launch.

The final scene showed Lassie working his way through a crowd watching the launch. My father embellished this scene by having Lassie start at the back of the crowd, then work his way to the front for a better view. That part wasn't in the script, but my father had better instincts than most actors.

In 1957, when Walt Disney decided it was time to cash in on America's love of dogs, he found that vehicle in *Old Yeller* (1957). It was the classic heartbreaking and heartwarming story of a boy and his dog. Disney veteran child actor Tommy Kirk played the lead. The young actress who could cry real tears on cue, Beverly Washburn, was hired as Tommy's child co-star. Fess Parker, Disney's Davy Crockett, came on-board, along with Dorothy McGuire, Jeff York, Chuck Connors, and a third child actor named Kevin Corcoran. Only one element was missing. Disney needed the canine star of the movie and a top-notch trainer.

At that time, my father was well-known throughout the movie and television industry. Some of the studios, like MGM, insisted on having him and no one else, provide and train their animal stars. Accepting every offer of work had become quite a challenge. Consequently, he hedged on the Disney project. He asked his brother, Frank, to provide one of his dogs and handle the studio work. A rescue from the pound named Spike was selected to be trained as Old Yeller, soon to be another iconic movie dog. I believe the cast all enjoyed working with Frank. Tommy Kirk and Beverly Washburn have fond memories of their time on the set with both Spike and Frank.

Years later I was asked to narrate the commentary for the DVD. Tommy Kirk was also part of this effort and I thoroughly enjoyed working with him. Prior to this recording, I had never seen *Old Yeller*. I told the DVD producer, but he didn't seem to mind. "Yes, but you know how it's done. You can watch it on the monitor and tell us all about what was happening and why." As the movie ran, I explained how Frank did the scenes with the dog. When we got to the scene with Spike and the wild boar fighting, I stumbled over my words. We staged fights between dogs but were able to control them with muzzles. In this scene, there was no reason to muzzle the dog, and boars fight with their horns. Frank knew his dog was young, large, and athletic enough to pull it off. It was a scary and exciting scene.

We never shied away from challenging situations. One such scene was filmed on a lake for a special titled *To Lassie With Love* (1974). We wanted to demonstrate how we worked the dog. In the scene, Lassie actually swims the lake while holding a cat. To accomplish this, a tether with a button attached to it was put under the cat's front legs. It was not visible because it was the same color as the cat's fur. Since Lassie was already trained to pick things up, all we had to do was show him the button and tell him to pick it up. Then we showed Lassie the cat wearing the tether with the button. When we filmed the scene, Lassie picked up the button attached to the harness, but it looked like he had the cat by the nape of the neck. I was positioned on the opposite side of the lake and called Lassie to swim toward me with the cat.

Not every collie is fit to work on a movie set. I used to joke with my father, "The good news is you get to work the most famous dog in the world. The bad news is it's a collie." When they become suspicious of noises or people, they investigate and stop paying attention to you. You can't blame the breed, as they were long ago bred to be very cautious and alert, not allowing predators to sneak up on the sheep they were herding. That was a serious drawback when it came to using such a dog in the context of a movie set and all the pandemonium that goes with it. Because of this, whenever we bred for another Lassie, there were puppies who were not destined for movie work. To my father they were just as precious as the Lassies themselves. Each and every one was given to a good home with strict criteria for their adoption. A potential owner had to have a yard with a fence around it and, most importantly, a good enough job so that we could be relatively certain the animal would be well-fed and cared for. Not just anyone received a puppy.

Many famous people got puppies from our litters. When I was eight years old, Margaret O'Brien wanted a dog. She qualified for a Weatherwax puppy and received a collie that was the last one in a litter. I played with all the dogs, but they weren't really my dogs. They were working dogs. During the qualification process Dad told her, "My son is giving you this dog."

When Margaret O'Brien and her mother came over to pick up the puppy, they arrived with a very large and expensive stuffed white monkey. It was a gift to me for supposedly giving up the puppy. I was quite shy then so I hid while the transaction took place. After they left, I wasted no time retrieving that monkey. I loved that stuffed toy and played with it a lot. One night I made a mistake and left the stuffed monkey in the yard. The next morning, it looked like snow was covering the ground. Dad let the dogs out and they had fun playing tug-of-war with that monkey, and my monkey was no more.

One of the most memorable puppy adoptions occurred during the Reagan administration. I was visiting my father in Malibu. Three vehicles with flags on the fender pulled up. Surprised, I said, "Dad, three limos just pulled up." Dad said, "That's Caspar Weinberger. I'm giving him a puppy, but it's no problem. He won't be here long." Caspar Weinberger, the Secretary of Defense, was coming to my father's home to pick up a puppy. The Secret Service was there with him. The agents got out of the cars and posted a guard at the gate to the property. As Dad opened the gate, one limo entered and drove up to the house. Out came the United States Secretary of Defense. Two men exited the limo with him and they guarded the doors. They were carrying Uzi submachine guns. I thought, *Man, I hope I don't sneeze or do something wrong to cause them to start shooting.* They looked like they really meant business.

I retrieved the puppy for my father, brought him into the room and put him down on the floor. Weinberger jumped down and sat there, crawling along with the dog. It sounded to me like he was talking baby talk to the puppy. *This is surreal,* I thought, *here we have the Secretary of Defense in our home and he's down on his hands and knees playing and cooing baby gibberish.*

Tex Ritter, who was a close friend of my father's, received a puppy. Years later, when I was working on the movie *Nickelodeon* (1976), his son John recalled his pet with great fondness. Liz Taylor was also supposed to get a puppy as a publicity stunt for the Universal show, *The*

New Lassie. Since we only bred when we needed a successor, we didn't have a real Lassie puppy to give her. I guess somebody just went out and presented her with a collie puppy. I don't know if she knew that or not.

Rudd Weatherwax was a brilliant man. The things he trained dogs to do and the skills he passed on to me, live on in the classic movies and television shows of which we were a part. Living and working with my father was not easy, but what he lacked in parenting skills, he more than made up in the training of dogs. Maybe brilliant people are not the easiest to live with.

Anne Sweeney, at the time an executive for Nickelodeon, came to my home to pick up a puppy for her sister. Sweeney said, "Your father taught animals to act better than most actors." This was a great compliment coming from her as she was an expert of entertainment involving children and animals. She later became an executive with Disney Studios.

17

Growing Up Weatherwax

THE FOURTH OF June is just an ordinary date on anyone's calendar. No one in the Weatherwax family had any reason to suspect that it had any particular significance. On June 4, 1940 Pal, the collie who was to become the star of *Lassie Come Home*, drew his first breath. Just one year later to the day in 1941, I took my place in the Weatherwax legend. Two new lives, born one year apart, would forever change this growing family's destiny. I was Dad's third child and Mom's second, named Robert Walter Weatherwax in honor of my grandfather. I grew up as Lassie's real life boy companion.

The first home I remember was a small white house that my father built himself with the help of some friends. It had one bedroom for my parents, a kitchen, and a bathroom off the kitchen. Adjacent to the kitchen was a tiny room with bunk beds for my sister and me. There was a small living room and the joke was that if you walked too fast you would walk into a wall.

When Lassie became a success, Dad bought a better home. That property didn't have kennels as large as he needed for his core business of providing dogs to the movie industry. For that reason, after the filming of the last MGM Lassie movies, our family moved back to our old home in North Hollywood. Dad built an addition which made the living room bigger and he painted it a nice shade of green, my mother's favorite color. It was still a small home.

Bob and his famous babysitter, Lassie

Dad rarely shared stories of his childhood, but the ones he did provided a great insight into his character. There are two stories Dad told me that illustrate the importance his father placed on personal strength.

Back in the New Mexico Territory, Walter was working at the kitchen table and Dad reached for something, accidentally knocking over his work. Walter reacted predictably and hit my father. Dad stood up as if he was going to fight. Walter challenged him, "You gonna stand up to me?" Thinking better of it, Dad headed for the door. Without warning, the iron his mother used to press his clothes was now streaking toward his head. My father never knew if Walter intended to put a dent in his head or was aiming for the door that now had a gaping hole. It didn't matter to Dad, the point was well taken. No one was to challenge the head of the family.

Bob eating breakfast with one of the cast of the Weatherwax kennels.

Walter also used sibling disputes as a tool to teach strength of character. Judd was the oldest child and my father was third from the youngest. The oldest brother was to lead the others and, like Walter, was never to be challenged. That rule was called into question many times among the brothers, as it was with Dad and Uncle Judd. Judd was usually the victor, but there was one time when Dad was getting the best of him. Walter was sitting on the porch watching the two brothers fight in the yard below. Walter noticed this turn of events and said to Judd, "If you let Rudd get the best of you then you're not my son." With that cruel taunt, Judd discovered a new surge of energy and Dad was totally deflated. Dad lost that battle and the natural order was restored.

My father raised his children the way he was raised. Everyone was taught responsibility.

When I was very young, he frequently used me as a prop to help train Pal, the original Lassie. I especially liked when Pal licked my face which was coated with baby food. That was how Lassie learned to kiss. That collie had the most beautiful, expressive eyes I have ever seen in a dog. My sister, Jo Ann, was used to teach Pal to snarl as he would have to do with Elizabeth Taylor. Lassie could snarl at someone and, in the next moment, give that same person a kiss. No matter what he was practicing, we all knew Pal would never hurt us.

As we got older, we were assigned more demanding jobs. Jo Ann had to take care of me and do the housework, as my mother was just too incapacitated at times. At the age of ten, I was assigned the task of caring for Dad's forty to fifty dogs. My father did not believe in hiring kennel help. Instead, he raised his own. Each morning before school, I trudged out to the kennel, fed and watered the canine crew, and cleaned up the area. It was a big responsibility and Dad was always there to remind me. Feeding and maintaining forty-four dogs before and after school, seven days a week, was not easy. Somehow I managed to get it all done.

My friends, on the other hand, didn't do much of anything. Nevertheless, their parents gave them a weekly allowance, around fifty cents a week. Once I asked Dad, "How come I don't get an allowance? All my friends are getting an allowance and I'm cleaning kennels and everything." My father had an answer ready, "I allow you to live." At least he said it with a smile. That was the kind of mindset the Weatherwax men had. It was as if he was still living in the Old West. In fact, he loved Westerns on TV so much that I used to joke about needing to dust off the TV because of all the horses riding by.

With allowances non-negotiable, I had to devise a clever way to make a little spending money. The kennel chores took up all of my time and the remoteness of our home made paper routes and lemonade stands unprofitable. I really needed to be creative. I came up with a scheme which required Dad to rent any of my personal pets that he might need on a project.

During the summer it was very hot in the yard when my father would be training Pal. Whenever Pal got tired, Dad would perk him up by showing him one of my hamsters. We negotiated a price of twenty-five cents per day for each hamster. I'd get paid at the end of the week. Now I believe that was Dad's way of making me earn an allowance. I inherited much of my mother's business acumen. I had no way of knowing that this was my first step down a career path of providing animals for the entertainment industry.

I rarely brought friends to my house. My sister and I recognized that our family life was far from normal. I never knew from day to day what I would find when I came home from school. Either my mother would be in the kitchen cooking one of her fabulous meals or she would be passed out on the couch, self-medicated with alcohol to treat what was likely a bipolar disorder. Sometimes she would still be in bed sleeping until the darkest part of her personality quieted and was put away until it appeared again. She would disappear into the bedroom for days at a time as if under a dark spell which, in a way, she was. I never knew if the evening would bring on another screaming match between my parents. We ate at a cheerless kitchen table fearing that, if I so much as spilled my milk, the swift justice of my father would be felt.

At twelve years of age, I converted the storage rooms above the garage into my bedroom, convincing my parents that I'd be nearer to my charges, the more than forty dogs I cared for. I'd be close to them at night so that if their sleep was disturbed by an errant skunk or other small animal, I'd be able to quiet the cacophony of barking animals. My room above the garage was my haven, my sanctuary. There I was safe, in a place where I could escape the turmoil that was a daily part of my home. At least there I didn't fear getting dragged out of bed in the middle of the night to referee one of my parents' frequent fights. Although it didn't happen often, I could hear if my father decided to seek me out by climbing the creaky steps to my room. Then I had plenty of time to escape through the window and sleep outside or in a car.

Although he excelled in what he did, Dad didn't have much of a formal education. He held his own set of beliefs and values, instilled by the stern hand of Walter Weatherwax. Never one to mince words or allude to what he meant, punishment for infractions was swift and sure in the Weatherwax household. Dad may have moved with his father to California, but they brought along with them the baggage of an unforgiving life in New Mexico.

When I grew older, I moved out for brief periods of time. The constant tension in our home often snapped as my mother threatened to leave. During those times I stayed with my sister. She was married by then, living first in Tennessee and later in Virginia. When I returned, my loft above the garage served as my refuge until we moved to the ranch in Sand Canyon.

Among the many dogs residing at the Weatherwax home, there was one who held a special rank. Pal did not live out in the kennel with the dogs I attended. Dad always kept his Lassie dogs with him inside our home, away from the others. Our home was Pal's castle, a special dog and my personal guardian. In fact, he once saved my life.

When I was a toddler, my parents couldn't afford a fence in the yard, so they would tether me to a tree to prevent me from running off. I quickly learned how to free myself by unhooking that harness and, one day, decided to take off and explore the great big world beyond the tree.

Our house on Van Owen was right off the street. Before long, I found myself in the middle of the road. Fortunately, there wasn't much traffic. Pal saw me and sensed that I was in danger and, within seconds, our famous collie was running toward me. He barked and nudged me with his nose, pushing me back toward the yard. My father heard the uproar and immediately knew something was wrong. As he watched Pal herding me, he hurried out to the street to retrieve us. Lassie not only saved lives on screen but also in real life. Before his heroics with Jeff or Timmy, I was the little boy actually rescued by Lassie.

My father's work and the need for the kennels required that we live in a relatively isolated area. My sister was a lot older than me and there were no kids in the neighborhood to play with. Needing companionship, I spent most of my day in the kennels with the dogs. Each day I chose a different dog to spend time with, especially when there was a litter. My mother started to worry when I mimicked the dogs by drinking out of their bowls. One of my favorite dogs in the kennels was named Dog. I called him Bulldog Sniff because he was in the first kennel and I could hear him snorting as I came in. Bulldog Sniff worked a lot. Before Dad took him on a job, he would get a block of ice for the car. There was no air-conditioning so Bulldog Sniff rode sitting on a blanket which covered the ice. This kept him cool.

With no other children around, the dogs became my army of soldiers and each one would be given a rank with periodic promotions. Pal, who lived in the house instead of the kennels, was the colonel because he was top dog. The working dogs were sergeants, corporals, and privates. The socialization was great for both me and the dogs. They enjoyed that time together as much as I did. They were my playmates and my brothers.

Every soldier must be neatly groomed and it was no different in my army. One bright and early day I found some scissors and decided to give Lassie a haircut. I didn't bother to tell my dad. I was looking forward to having some fun with our dog.

First, I cut off his black tassels which are very slow-growing fur alongside the ears. I thought about cutting the hair off his tail but I didn't know where the hair left off and the tail began. I was worried that I'd cut part of his tail. Leaving the tail alone was one of the wisest decisions I made that morning.

When my father rose from bed, he strolled into the living room and saw the results of Little Bob's Canine Barber Shop. He did not seem very happy. It looked to me as if storm clouds were rolling over his face. I was quickly relieved of duty and moved as far away from Lassie as one could possibly get. I always wondered why my father never punished me for the haircut. Years later, he said he probably would have killed me.

Those black tassels take a very long time to grow back and Dad's star dog was scheduled to start a new movie very soon. In the make-believe land of Hollywood, all things are possible. My father visited the studio hair stylist that week and he soon came home with specially designed black tassel hairpieces. Pal would have to wear a wig in his next movie, thanks to me. Like Elvis, he lost his beautiful hair to the demands of the Army.

Lassie's army training also involved self-defense. With all the pine cones laying around our yard I thought they would be good to use on Lassie for target practice. Both my mother and father happened to be inside the house watching and my mother asked, "Aren't you going to stop him?" My father was unconcerned. "Don't worry. Lassie will take care of him." Sure enough, I hit Lassie with one of the pine cones and he went into full attack mode. He charged me, knocked me down, and straddled me. He put his muzzle to within a few inches of my face and snarled. He then just walked away and continued what he was doing. At that point, my father came out and I thought I was going to get punished. As I waited for my court-martial, my father said, "No, I'm not going to punish you, because Lassie took care of the situation." My father knew that Lassie taught me a lesson I would never forget.

Bud Ekins, who was a stuntman for Steve McQueen, was Dad's nephew, the son of my father's sister, Peggy. He was best known for his work in the movie *The Great Escape* (1963). He was also one of the greatest motocross racers of all time and my father loved to go and watch him race. When I was ten or eleven years old, Dad usually took me along for company as he never liked traveling alone and Mom did not want to go. It became a way for us to bond.

Bud wasn't just a good racer, he always won by ridiculous margins. He crossed the finish line, smoked one of his French cigarettes, and had a shot of scotch, all while waiting for the second place racer to come along. He quipped, "Yeah I guess he'll be along pretty soon. I passed him about an hour ago." He was in a class all by himself.

When I got out of the Army I didn't have much money. Instead of a car, I bought my first motorcycle, a Honda, since it was cheaper transportation. I later traded the Honda to Bud for a Triumph which I converted into a dirt bike. Because of Bud, I started racing. I would sometimes race against him. He was past his prime, but still better than most. I was good, but never in Bud's class. In his later years he was racing because he was trying to sell a motorcycle called a Rickman. My father started to come out to watch me race. Sometimes we slept overnight in the back of my van. During one race, I came into the pits to get some gas. Bud was behind me. I heard my father yell to him, "See Bud, my son is beating you!" Later Bud passed me, but it was one of the few times my father expressed pride in me.

Since the very earliest days of the industry, alcohol has reigned as the drug of choice for hard-working, hard-driving motion picture people. It didn't matter whether one was a major star or a production assistant. The long hours and pressure of putting a film project together, on time and within budget, created a pressured atmosphere for everyone involved. The veterans had a name for the last shot before wrapping up for the day. They called it the martini shot.

It seemed almost preordained that Dad eventually found solace from the bottle, whether at home or at The Rag Doll. Frank Inn used to say that when my father became too intoxicated, he also became a little too exuberant. I came to understand what Frank meant when I first saw my father ride a horse into the house. I could still picture him riding through the den and out onto the patio where the horse bucked and threw him ten feet into the air. It was nighttime and all I could see was his white shirt going up in the air. As that white streak landed on the ground, I wondered what would have happened if that horse had bucked in the house with the low ceiling. He likely would have broken his neck.

We had a few cattle in the pasture behind our home. They were not used for movies. They were there so the dogs would become accustomed to them and not be afraid of the same type of animal on a movie set. Dad's friends came over some nights, got drunk and, looking for something to do, staggered to the back yard to ride the steers. Not welcoming the riders, they bucked, throwing them in every direction. One landed on the barbed wire fence. At the end of the impromptu rodeo, most of the wannabe cowboys limped their way back to the house. The next morning, my sister and I would traipse out to the field and pick up all the change that had fallen out of the riders' pockets. Half dollar coins were popular and were much better than quarters or dimes. We always split the money, sometimes finding as much as five dollars in change. Money was tight in those days and I welcomed any source of income. My sister and I loved rodeo nights.

When our guests were not in the rodeo mood they liked to play catch, with me as the ball. Dad showed me how to curl up and they tossed me back and forth. Occasionally someone attempted to show off their strength by lifting me with one arm before staggering into the couch. This may sound strange today but it was the 1940s in Hollywood where everyone worked hard and played hard. Despite my mother's objections, they thought it was normal behavior and so did I.

Herman Salmon was a test pilot who frequently visited our house. With a name like Salmon, it was obvious for him to have adopted the nickname of Fish. Dad and Fish would down a few rounds of liquid refreshment and then look for ways to express themselves, usually with a shotgun. Additional pellets would find their way into the ceiling which was already peppered from previous shootings.

The house was often damaged, the recipient of abuse by the inebriated occupants. In our garage was stacked extra glass for the windows on the house. It was a regular occurrence for someone to be fighting and break a window. Dad fought with his brother, Frank, sometimes rolling around the kitchen floor. Many times one of them put an elbow through a window. Dad and my brother Jackie also fought a lot like that, as would many of our drunken guests. We should have been called The Fighting Weatherwaxes. They never left the Wild West days totally behind.

Dad's descent into alcoholism derived primarily from the stress caused by the movie and television industry, but the animals themselves also caused their share. Having the dogs perform multiple tasks with the many distractions of a movie set was difficult, especially with collies. The breed is not naturally suited for that environment. Dad found a way to do all this, but it took a heavy toll on his personal life. In addition to the stress originating from the training regimen, there were worries about the dogs' health. An illness or accident could be devastating. His anxiety was heightened, trying to protect his dogs not only because they were his livelihood but also because he loved them so much. There was a deep emotional attachment. They were my father's entire life and there was little room for anything or anyone else.

At times, the emotional burden of dealing with my mother and her mental health problems also caused Dad concern, along with his ever present fear of losing everything. We were enjoying a lifestyle that surpassed anything that he had ever imagined possible. The hardships of his early life were never far from his thoughts and he was always prepared for their return, as was my mother. She wore house dresses that cost two dollars, always waiting for the next Great Depression.

This frame of mind no doubt triggered his need for stress release, and he found it in alcohol and gambling. He felt invigorated by both. Over time, the things that gave him relief became sources of conflict. My father was known to the world as the original owner and trainer of

Lassie, but he owned his share of personal demons as well. Those demons seemed to thrive in the hearts and souls of many of Hollywood's most successful people. Perhaps they were occupational hazards.

As I look back on the days of growing up in my home, it reminds me of the famous opening line of Charles Dickins' *A Tale of Two Cities*: "It was the best of times, it was the worst of times…" There is no better way to describe my childhood and my relationship with my parents. I was privileged to be part of a family legacy that made movie history, and forced to pay the price by surrendering the comfort of a loving home. I had to find my solace outside, with the animals that I cared for, and in the room above the garage that kept me close to them. It was not ideal, but it was all part of growing up Weatherwax.

18

A Father's Legacy

TOWARD THE END of his life, my father worried about his legacy. He often wondered if the legend of Lassie should die with him, fearing that someone coming after him would damage the dog's image. In the end he left Lassie VII, his last, to me. Dad devoted his life to that legacy. He knew he couldn't do the work forever and he did not know that I would eventually take over. In Hollywood, as in life, situations change rapidly and plans are often just the things of dreams.

My father envisioned that my brother, Jackie, would be the one to continue the tradition of Lassie after he was gone. Jackie was earmarked by our father to follow in his footsteps, to become a great dog trainer like his dad. Although their intentions are most times good and valid, sometimes what parents think is best for their children is not at all the proper direction. That was so with Jackie who preferred cleaning pools, a job my father considered rather mundane. However, it was the perfect job for him, one that he enjoyed immensely. He was not pressured and he was able to spend most of his time outdoors. In the entertainment industry, pressure is as much a part of the job as breathing the air around us. Being forced into something that one neither has an interest in nor any innate ability can be corrupting to the spirit.

Time and time again, Dad hired Jackie for jobs that he was incapable of doing. Dad never gave up and his tenacity in this case proved to be most unfortunate. Jackie liked to drink and this caused a problem. Sometimes he slept in the car while my father was working and I was there to help out. One such day, Bill Beaudine Jr, the production manager, came up to my father and said, "I want Jackie fired and Bob hired." My father said to him, "You can't do that. I'm the head of this department." Bill said, "Yes, but I write the checks and I'm not going to write any more checks for him to stay in the car all day."

Whether by nature or nurture, Jackie was deeply troubled. This manifested itself often in horrific behavior, sadly at times, directed at me or the animals. Jackie himself was not immune to the wrath of his maleficence. My half-brother died as the result of doing a "James Dean" around a hairpin turn on a narrow road in the canyons. He was intoxicated at the time, a not uncommon state for Dad's first born. He lingered for several months before he finally succumbed to the injuries he sustained. That time, instead of taking out his anger on others, he turned it inward and hurt himself irreparably.

Alcoholism was unquestionably taking its toll on Dad. His feelings of guilt were crushing his soul. Self-reproach to the extreme seemed to have been in his genes. He could not forgive himself for the death of his first wife, after forcing her out of the house. The day my father threw an intoxicated Jackie out of the house was the day his first son and designated successor headed for that fatal hairpin turn.

I believe that the collies who Dad trained to perform as Lassie took on human attributes for a very unique and unusual reason. My father grew up in a family devoid of any expression of emotion and human compassion and, as a result, found it difficult to exhibit them himself. I don't think anyone ever expressed emotion in our house. If they did, it wasn't positive emotion.

Dad found a different outlet for his feelings and emotions. He conveyed them through his dogs. In a scene in which Lassie comes in and kisses the child, it's heartwarming. It's also Rudd Weatherwax channeling his own repressed feelings in a way he found acceptable. Dad could deal with the dog, but not with people. The dog was safe. Through the dog, my dad could love and be loved in return. He could communicate those feelings which he could not express to any other person. That's what made those collies so great. The dogs were really Rudd Weatherwax with long hair and four paws.

My father put his life and soul into creating the image of a fictional dog named Lassie. "Always protect that dog's image." That permeated my life from the day I was born. No studio could have protected its star as Dad protected the public persona of Lassie. He put the dog out front never taking credit for his talent. If someone observed, "You must spend a lot of time training that dog, Mr. Weatherwax," Dad would reply, "Why, no. Lassie is a very smart dog." I once asked him why he would say that. His answer came easy, "You never compete with your commodity. Lassie is what they want, Lassie is what I give them. It has to be this way." Lassie got the accolades no matter where we went. I once found a briefcase in Central Park while we were walking Lassie and Dad proudly announced, "Lassie found it."

Rudd relaxing with his favorite companion.

Dad's work with the dogs was the real love of his life. He made fortunes beyond belief for a number of people in both the movie and television industries yet, in the end, he could not afford to buy a house he wanted. He may have had a very comfortable lifestyle, but he was short on the receiving end when credits and compensation were given out for Lassie. The TV show made mega millions and, over nineteen years, won its share of Emmys and Peabody Awards. Despite all this success, true Hollywood fame and fortune eluded Dad.

My father never indicated that he was bitter about his financial situation. He made so many people fabulously rich, and perhaps he felt well-off when thinking back about the hardscrabble days in the New Mexico Territory. Whenever I asked about the unfairness of the financial situation, Dad would always respond, "I only want to work my dog."

Toward the end of his life my father's attitude changed. Reporters from *Entertainment Tonight* came to interview him. They stated, "Mr.

Weatherwax, you must be very rich." He objected, "No, I made a lot of other people rich, but not me." The young interviewer repeatedly told my father where to look into the camera. I could see the contempt he had for this reporter, and he said sarcastically, "Yeah? You think I should look over there? Really? I didn't know that!" That was the last interview he ever did. He received a request from an organization to appear in five years to receive an award. He asked me, "Do they know how old I am? Do they really think I'll be around by then?" He committed to it but passed away before the event. I agreed to go in his place. It was presented on *Good Morning America* with David Hartman, but I don't recall much about receiving the award. It was too early after losing my father and I was emotionally numb.

The chaos that seemed to follow my father left him with a nagging guilt that persisted throughout his life. Deep in his soul he knew that some of his actions hurt other people, and he was aware that somehow, despite his faults, fate had rewarded him with great success.

In 1962, my parents divorced. By then, Dad's gambling was as much a problem as the alcohol. My mother was concerned that the TV series wouldn't last much longer. With Dad's gambling habit, she believed they would end up broke. My father gave Mom a $250,000 property settlement and she gave him the complete rights to Lassie.

A year later, in 1963, my father married his third and last wife, Betty Brooks. It was a relatively tranquil marriage, at least by Weatherwax standards. There was strife, however, and their last time together was spent fighting. In 1977, while Dad was filming *The Magic of Lassie* (1978), Betty died. His remorse led him to mitigate his self-determined culpability by leaving her children a share of the Lassie trademark equal to his own two children. My father's guilt was usually accompanied by compassion and generosity.

Material things never meant much to my father. He would invite people to our house and, if they were impressed by some award or piece of Lassie memorabilia laying around, he would simply tell them to take it. As a result of a house fire, my father lost countless, invaluable artifacts accumulated over a great Hollywood career. The house and its contents were a total loss but no one, animals included, was harmed. While the rest of us were distraught over the lost possessions, Dad just waved his hand dismissively and said, "Those things don't matter." All he really cared about was training his star dog. Even a burning house could not light a different fire in his heart.

Few people have heard about the Rudd Weatherwax who genuinely cared about people. When we were in New York, Dad, Sam Williamson, and I often walked Lassie in Central Park. Before going out, Dad always grabbed a stack of twenty-dollar bills to take with him. Before long, he would find the homeless lying on benches. Most of them were passed out or asleep. Dad would approach them silently and stuff their pockets with the money. I can only imagine their surprise when they woke up and found those twenty-dollar bills. If they were awake, he would simply give it to them. Sam worried about Dad's routine, explaining that we could get mugged. It was a dangerous thing to do especially for, what Sam felt, were undeserving bums. "They don't deserve this," he scolded my father. Dad pointed out, "Not necessarily. Except for that fork in the road, that could've been me on that bench."

Those generous cash handouts were not easy for him. One of his looming demons was the fear of regressing back to the days of financial struggles. Still, he stiffened his psychological backbone and went out, frequently and anonymously, to help the poor. I think they reminded him of where he had once been in life, down and out. The struggles of New Mexico were always with him. Rudd Weatherwax, despite his personal shortcomings, changed the world and made it a better place for us all. He was a man who knew how to, in his words, "pay it back." When someone approached Dad for a loan, he always gave it to them without expecting repayment. He observed, "If a man has to borrow a thousand dollars and is barely making it on the salary he is earning, how do you think he'll ever be able to repay that loan? He won't. Maybe, somewhere down the line, he'll be in a position to help someone else in need." That was the Rudd Weatherwax philosophy of life. For all his faults, Dad lived by those words. Of all the famous people Dad met during his lifetime, one person stood out among all the others, Mother Teresa. When she asked for permission to pet Lassie, he granted it willingly. He considered meeting this modern day saint one of the highlights of his life.

Rudd Weatherwax also had a special place in his heart for children in dire circumstances. He required that a clause be included in his personal appearance contracts stating that when he was traveling with Lassie doing live performances, he would be allowed to stop at the local children's hospital. He believed a personal appearance by Lassie could actually help the healing process with the little patients. These were not easy for him and they all took an emotional toll on Dad, yet he believed in his heart that they were something he was preordained to do. The visits gave a new, rich meaning and purpose to his life. "It's my church," he would say.

Lassie visiting a children's hospital.

There was an especially heart-wrenching visit we made to a large hospital. The woman who greeted us at the door asked if we could immediately go to a room upstairs, where a child with leukemia was near death. We had the very hyperactive Hey Hey with us and were a little worried because the child had hoses and other medical apparatus attached. I imagined Hey Hey acting like a big clunk, getting excited and putting his paws on the child and the equipment. Somehow, the collie sensed that this child was not well and he gently put his feet up on that bed, as if they were on eggs. That dog actually knew how to comfort a dying child and sensed he had to be gentle with this boy. He put his paw up and placed his head carefully near the boy so that the child could reach out and touch the real Lassie. Aware of all of this, he smiled and petted the dog. He and Hey Hey experienced a few minutes of bonding as only a boy and a dog could. We then visited the other young patients in the hospital, all of whom expressed a similar joy.

As we were leaving, the woman who originally greeted us deliv-ered the crushing news that the little boy had passed away. Among his last thoughts were his minutes with the world's most famous collie. Our Lassies did some heroic things in real life.

My father passed away on February 25, 1985. As he was dying, he worried about the image of the dog he loved and nurtured. That's how dedicated he was to Lassie. As his days came to an end, all he wanted was to see his dogs again. I regretted that my sister called an ambu-lance and he was not allowed to die at home, surrounded by what he loved most. His last moments should have included his dogs. As he was leaving this world, he could have reached out and touched them one last time, like that little boy we met in the hospital. For not pro-viding him with this opportunity, I am deeply sorry to this day.

Rudd and Lassie at home

Dad was raised as a Catholic, although he was not a practicing Catholic throughout his life. He referred to himself as a "deathbed Catholic," clinging to some of the beliefs he was taught as a child, "just in case." At his funeral I instructed the priest not to say that dogs don't go to heaven. I believed that if there is such a place, our dogs would have to be there too. My father never would have wanted to go where he couldn't be with his dogs.

The torch had now passed from father to son. As difficult as it was to accept, the sun had set on a Weatherwax legend. When it rose again the next day, it would be me holding the flame.

19

The Son Also Rises

MY FATHER PASSED away while I was working on *Back to the Future* (1985). I didn't want to talk to anybody so I told my assistant to fill in for me. If they needed the dog he could work him and I would be available if there was a difficult scene. We filmed mostly at night for this movie and spent some of this time merely waiting until a scene required my dog. Barely able to function, I was not emotionally ready to deal with anyone trying to console me over his loss.

Producer Steven Spielberg sent a beautiful note and flowers. The day I buried my father, my mentor and good friend, Sam Williamson, died. Sam had been Dad's faithful assistant for so long that it was hard to imagine a world in which Rudd Weatherwax and Sam Williamson no longer existed. Sam was really like family to us.

I think the gods were determined to make the year 1985 unbearable for me. Within months of burying my father and Sam, my best friend died of a massive heart attack. Ron Oxley, best known for his bear in *Gentle Ben*, was working on a show titled *Project X*, which was released in 1987. He came to my house the evening he died. We ate dinner, he went home to bed and he never woke up. Sometimes I wonder if the pressures from that show were what actually killed him. I felt guilty about that since I helped him get that job.

With three devastating losses in such a short amount of time, I found myself reflecting about where I had been, where I was, and where I was going. By the time my father passed away, I had a successful business and had become a respected trainer in my own right. I learned a lot working with Dad and Sam Williamson, but conducting my own business was quite a journey, one that would eerily find me traveling the same path as my father.

I acquired my skills over a long period of time, starting soon after I was discharged from the Army. Working with my father, and under the calming direction of Sam Williamson, I began to work on the *Lassie* series. My father had many friends in the business, one of his closest was Frank Barnes who did the show, *Rin Tin Tin*. Dad and I visited the set once in a while and he and Frank would often socialize. They enjoyed playing games with their dogs, sort of a friendly competition. One they enjoyed was taking their dogs to houses that were still under construction to see whose dog could find the bathroom first. Frank would win because he taught his dog to go to the smallest room. That was his secret.

Frank Barnes had a dog named Bearheart. Frank Inn was working the *Daniel Boone* series, starring Fess Parker. Bearheart was used in an episode of the series. Frank Inn's trainer on the set was Karl Miller. It was there that I first worked with Karl as his helper. I was contracted for three days to assist him with a dog that Frank Barnes trained. I knew a lot about Bearheart because of my father's friendship with Barnes. Karl was unaware that Bearheart was trained using a rubber ball. He was one of the dogs on the *Rin Tin Tin* show and I knew the technique. Needless to say, Karl was quite impressed with my results. He went back to Frank Inn and told him that he wanted me to assist him with everything. Frank told him, "He won't be here to assist you on everything!" I had only been hired to work for three days, but at least I felt appreciated.

I started having some of my own dogs perform on other TV shows. One of my collies, Silver, who was in *Big Jake,* starred in an episode of *The Odd Couple,* "The Dog Story." The plot had Felix kidnapping a famous dog star from his abusive owner. I won a PATSY award for Silver's performance and he went on to star with James Arness in an episode of *Gunsmoke,* proving that a collie didn't have to be Lassie to be a solid performer.

After a nineteen-year run, we were about to film the last episode of *Lassie.* My father wanted me to do this episode with my dog Silver. Hey Hey, who played Lassie at the time, had a shoulder injury and was limping. I also think he wanted to showcase my talents for Frank Inn. Frank Inn had a dog featured in this final episode named Higgins. Higgins was the dog on *Petticoat Junction* and later attained fame as Benji. This episode was the last one filmed, although it may not have been the last one broadcast. There was a scene where Silver and Higgins had to walk down the road together. I could get Silver to do it, but Frank had yet to teach Higgins how to follow commands from a distance. He asked, "How are we going to do this scene?" I came up with the idea of tethering the dogs to each other using monofilament looped around each dog's neck. In that way, when I called Silver, Higgins had no choice but to walk with Silver. It worked. Sam, my father's assistant, overheard Frank comment, "I think Bob is as good or better than his father was at this age and as good as him now." I told Sam that was because "I read the book." I was building on what my father had learned and taught me. He developed his training method over all those years, by trial and error, and now I was the beneficiary. When I was a boy, I had seen my father training the dogs in the back yard and thought nothing of it. All that changed the day I first went on the set and saw how he worked the dog and set up a scene. I thought, *Boy, I really like this. This is what I want to do.*

After the original *Lassie* TV series wrapped, I became a driver for about a year, since, as a trainer for the *Lassie* show, I belonged to the Teamsters Union. I didn't really like driving very much. By this time, Sam Williamson was working for an animal supplier named Lou Schumacher. Sam wasn't happy with his job either. Sam lived in La Jolla and was not thrilled with the long commute. Lou told Sam he could move in with him, but Sam was convinced that nothing short of a replacement would do. When Sam made his pitch, Lou was reluctant to even consider me. Sam assured him that I was as good as my dad and I could do the job. That was what Lou needed to hear and Sam was soon free to move on.

Many of Lou's dogs were not trained properly so I used every technique I knew to retrain them to get through their scenes. Some of those scenes were quite dangerous, especially for the actors. One of the first projects I was assigned was with a German shepherd named Concho. The movie was appropriately titled *The Strange and Deadly Occurrence* (1974).

The first thing I noticed when I met Concho was that he wanted to devour me. My top priority in training that dog was to make sure he did not start to salivate every time he saw me. When I got to the point where I felt reasonably safe with him, my next thought concerned the actors. I was unsure of how he would interact with them.

The script called for Concho to be tied to a fence. As Robert Stack and Vera Miles approached the house, the dog was to bark and carry on. There was not supposed to be any human contact. When we went to shoot the scene, the director changed everything around. Instead, he wanted the dog to ride in a car with the actors. The script called for Miles and Stack to get out of the car with the dog on a leash. As they walked up to the villain, the dog was supposed to freak out. Then the actors were to kneel down and try to calm the raging dog, who genuinely viewed actors as kibble. My first thought was whether Hollywood could survive the loss of both Vera Miles and Robert Stack.

Vera Miles was the first one to fear for her life. "I'm not kneeling down. I don't like the looks of that dog." Robert Stack recalled that he had been bitten by a lion early in his career. I previously told the director that Concho was dangerous and had already tried to bite me. "We could end up getting someone hurt with those script revisions." The director turned to me and said, "Let me worry about that. We'll have a bloody go at it!" I said, "Yep, that's exactly what we may have, a bloody go!"

My first concern before the cameras rolled was not the actors but rather the boom microphone. Concho had been stick trained so that pole would have been the most mammoth stick he could possibly have enjoyed attacking. I covered his eyes as the boom operator put the equipment in place. Next, I introduced Concho to the two actors.

Concho had been trained to get excited with the stick and calm down when a chain was thrown to the ground. Filming began and the car came into the scene and the actors got out. When Concho saw the villain, I showed him the stick and he got highly agitated. When the actors bent down to calm him, I threw the chain down. Right on cue, Concho calmed down and the scene was a success. I was thankful that it all worked out. If two top actors had been bitten on my watch, I never would have worked in Hollywood again.

Lou Schumacher later assigned me to work on the movie *Nickelodeon* (1976), starring Ryan O'Neal, Burt Reynolds, and a young John Ritter. Peter Bogdanovich directed it. Lou was in trouble on the film because his dog wouldn't perform. I was the fourth trainer sent to the project. The previous three were fired by the director who was threatening to sue. Lou promised he would send me, his best dog trainer, to shoot the scenes. Before Lou sent me, he failed to mention the chaos that had already broken out on the set.

When I arrived, I discovered that the dog working on the film had been traumatized and was shaking. A prop man asked me if the dog needed a blanket. I told him that the animal wasn't cold, he was scared to death. Earlier he had gotten hurt in a scene in which Tatum O'Neal was driving a car. I had yet to unpack my bags and was waiting for someone to say the wrong thing. I would not have hesitated to walk off. I must have had an angry look on my face because I overheard Ryan O'Neal say to Burt Reynolds, "I don't know who this new dog trainer is but I'm not going to say anything to him. He looks like he would kill you!"

John Ritter, who apparently did not perceive me as a violent man, came over and said, "Your father gave me a puppy when I was a little boy. He was my childhood pet and was with me when I was growing up." John's father was Tex Ritter, the legendary country singer. He and my father were very good friends. I said, "Good, John. Now you have to help me out. I need someone in the scene to be with the dog so he won't be afraid. Just snap his leash and then give him a treat. He'll go with you." John was happy to help and, since he was in many scenes requiring the dog, it worked exactly as planned.

The running gag in the script was that the dog liked to bite everyone's legs. There was one scene in which Ryan O'Neal ran and jumped over a small pile of dirt in the middle of a big empty field. The dog was to chase him, jump over the same pile of dirt, and bite O'Neal's leg. The dog's natural inclination would be to run around the pile, so it was a very difficult scene. I positioned myself fifty yards ahead of the dog and had the assistant director release him when I called. The dog did exactly as the script required and Bogdanovich was happy with the job I did. When Lou Schumacher tried to pull me off the job to work on *Won Ton Ton: The Dog Who Saved Hollywood* (1976), producer Frank Marshall told him that he would sue. Marshall finally had someone who could work the dog and he wasn't about to let me go.

I was gaining the reputation of fixing things that were broken. One thing I couldn't fix, however, were runaway ostriches. We were working outside of Hollywood in Ventura on a big ranch. There was a scene that included ostriches supplied by my friend, Ron Oxley. Ron had the birds corralled and he warned everyone not to leave the gate open whenever they went into that area. The birds would be very hard to catch if they got out. They can run at about thirty-five miles per hour. No one listened to Ron and, sure enough, someone left the gate open. Three of the ostriches decided to run for their lives. I don't want to repeat Ron's exact words but, basically, he made it clear that somebody had better get the birds back.

Hal Needham was Burt Reynolds' stunt double. I was friends with Hal from our membership in a studio motorcycle racing club called The Viewfinders which consisted mostly of stuntmen. Hal thought he had a plan. He jumped in his rented Mercedes and drove across the field after one of the birds. As he caught up to it, he flung open the driver's side door in an attempt to trap it. Instead, the bird ran through the door and ripped it right off the hinges. I wondered what Hal was going to tell the rental company about how the door got torn off. I had a picture in my mind of Hal driving home in a Mercedes missing a front door.

Most stunt doubles are fairly anonymous people in Hollywood. Hal Needham was the exception. While his day job was performing dangerous stunts, Hal aspired to write and produce his own movies. He developed one that none of the studios showed any interest in at all. Hal had the clever idea of asking his friend, Burt Reynolds, to sign a letter of intent to appear in the movie. Burt was a superstar and his name on the project opened the studio gates. Hal Needham realized his dream and became a Hollywood producer, writer, and director with the hit film *Smokey and the Bandit* (1977).

The strain of working with someone else's poorly trained dogs was starting to take its toll on me. I didn't see any future in going out on difficult and dangerous jobs with Lou Schumacher's dogs. In 1976, I decided to start my own business, Weatherwax Trained Dogs. I sold my house and moved to a location where the zoning would allow kennels. I purchased my business license and started visiting the dog pounds. The search for the next group of Weatherwax entertainment animals had begun. In order to survive financially and pay the bills, my next order of business was to develop a clientele. Success in Hollywood depends upon a solid reputation by proving you can deliver whatever is needed. I got a boost when I landed the movie *Moment by Moment* (1978) with John Travolta and Lily Tomlin. The movie had the same producer as *Grease* (1978). One day, Olivia Newton-John came to visit the set. We were doing the movie with my little white Maltese, Scamp. Olivia saw him, came running over, and gave him a big kiss on his nose. That was okay with Scamp, but it left a huge lipstick stain on him and we had to delay the shoot to get him cleaned off.

That movie gave me a steady income for four months and helped me build the business. Later, I was fortunate to obtain long-term work on the television series, *Simon and Simon*. These two early successes laid the foundation for a thriving business.

I had the opportunity to work with and meet many wonderful people, one of my favorites being Michael Landon. He was very good to his crew. When he was producing *Little House on the Prairie*, he brought over the best and most efficient people from *Bonanza*. He was a perfectionist and had very high standards. At Christmastime, crew members would find two or three thousand dollars extra in their paychecks.

The first time I worked with Michael Landon was with a dog that was playing a wolf. Our first meeting was not a good one. The moment he saw me, he started running up the hill screaming, "I told you if I ever saw you again, I was going to knock you out!" I thought to myself, *What is this all about?* I didn't know who was running toward me but I estimated that by the time he got to me, he would be out of breath and I could hit him first. When he got about fifty feet away from me, he paused and said, "Wait a minute! You're not the guy I thought you were." Mike thought I was the dog trainer that he had fired earlier. I picked up a lot of business from trainers who had failed and couldn't make their dogs perform in a way that the directors needed. To cover their retreat from the project, many would say, "Oh, I'm going to send you Bob Weatherwax. He is a miracle worker." I always appreciated the compliment, but it meant that I would get exceptionally challenging assignments in which the previous trainer already failed. It was non-stop pressure.

The next time I worked with Michael Landon was on another episode of *Little House on the Prairie* called "No Beast So Fierce" which featured Buck, my white shepherd. The script required the dog to snarl in the boy's face. There was some trepidation about doing this scene. "Is it safe?" they asked me. I assured them that the boy was in no danger although it took a certain amount of courage for him to put his face inches away from a snarling dog. One of the actors said, "You got a great dog there." Then he turned around and said, "And you're not so bad yourself."

Michael Landon was a wonderful, down-to-earth person with a solid work ethic. A great example of his character was reflected in his willingness to help others. One part of the script called for the dog to escape by digging under a fence. The ground was hard and, in reality, it would take hours for a dog to dig like that. I suggested digging a hole before filming. The hole could then be filled with loose dirt, which the dog could easily and quickly dig up. Usually one of the laborers would do this kind of job, but on that day none of them were there so I started digging the hole myself. Not long afterward, I heard a shovel working the dirt next to me. At first I thought it was one of the crew, but when I looked up it was Michael Landon. There he was, digging right alongside me. That's the kind of guy he was. If you did your job right, Mike was always there to help out.

I had the opportunity to work on the movie, *The Magic of Lassie* (1978), which starred James Stewart, Stephanie Zimbalist, Pernell Roberts, and Mickey Rooney. The score was written by the highly successful songwriting brothers, Richard and Robert Sherman, who listed among their numerous credits the Disney classic, *Mary Poppins* (1964). Their title song, "When You're Loved," was sung by Debby Boone. It garnered an Academy Award nomination for "Best Original Song." My father had been contracted to do the movie but his third wife Betty died suddenly during the production, postponing filming for two weeks. He tried to come back but could no longer continue the project. His grief was too much to bear and, as a result, his drinking increased.

The studio contacted me to see if I would complete the movie. By then I had a thriving business and had no interest in taking over Lassie. Financially it made no sense. I made demands I thought they would reject, but to my surprise they agreed to everything I asked for in order to get me to take the project. Consequently, I took the job and had to hire another trainer to cover my own projects.

The Magic of Lassie was shown at Radio City Music Hall. For six weeks, following each showing, we did a live stage performance with Lassie. The movie also inspired the concept of a new television show and Dad was hired to do the pilot. The show was never sold.

Dad once told me something I will never forget. "You are a good trainer so you will train a lot of great dogs. There will be one outstanding dog that none other will ever match." That dog for me was OJ. He was indeed my very special dog. In the training business, sometimes you are called to fix a difficult problem and having a dog like OJ can change panic into applause.

Harvey Korman was scheduled to do a live skit on *The Tim Conway Show*. I got a last minute call asking if I had a dog that would sit on a box and tug on a rag. Most dogs will not play tug-of-war with you while they are standing on top of a box, much less while sitting on it. The skit called for someone to carry a pair of pants across the stage in front of the live audience. They had hired another trainer to do this but he didn't work out. The show was scheduled to begin in a few hours.

"Can you get the dog to do that?"

"Sure."

"Get over there right away."

I was with Sam Williamson, my father's assistant, and he seemed quite worried. When we were alone he expressed his concerns.

"Bob, you are never going to be able to do that."

"Sam, you don't know OJ."

"Bob, it's going to take some preparation, especially if they want the dog to drag those pants all the way to the end of the stage."

By show time it was do or die. In Hollywood, you have to exude confidence and assure clients that you can do the job. You never, ever falter. That's when you lose an opportunity. Later on, after you are back home, you can marvel at your audacity and the fact that you pulled off the near impossible.

The opening called for the dog to tug on some pants. We set it up so that my hands were on the pants, but out of the picture. The dog would be pulling on the other end. Then Harvey Korman was supposed to come onstage and yell, "Hey, that dog is stealing my pants."

Sam said OJ would never do that. He predicted that by the time the
dog got to the end of the stage he would drop those pants. That's when
my bravado reached its peak. I boasted, "Not only will OJ perform
exactly as we want, but he will also do something else that will put this
scene over the top."

OJ

Show time in front of the live audience soon arrived. There would be no retakes. Harvey Korman came through the door. OJ lined right up with Harvey and offered him the pants. This was unexpected. When Harvey tried to take the pants away from him, OJ engaged in a playful tug-of-war and the actor was pleasantly surprised. Their lively contest of who would get the pants continued all the way across the stage. By this time the audience was going crazy. It was a showstopper. The producer came up to me and said, "I want you and your dog to take a bow." I turned to Sam and said, "Hey Sam. What do you think of OJ now?"

I met with Steven Spielberg to audition OJ for the role of Einstein, the dog in *Back to the Future* (1985). Spielberg was sitting behind his desk and had a long shelf that ran the length of the wall, at the end of which was a pot of flowers. "Is this dog well-trained?" Steven asked. "Of course," I replied. "Well if he's that smart, have him go to the end of this shelf and smell those flowers." OJ was already trained to respond to the words *go* and *nudge*. I told OJ, "Go," and cued him until he positioned himself in line with the flowers. Then, with the same inflection I used for the word *nudge*, I said, "Smell." OJ stopped in line with the flowers and appeared to smell them. Spielberg was amazed. "You can't do that again," he said, as he moved the flower. By now the dog had learned the trick. All I had to do was tell OJ, "Go and smell the flower." He went right up and smelled the flower. Spielberg was smiling. "Which Weatherwax brother is your father?" "Rudd," I responded. "Oh, he's the one who did Lassie. Your father is a genius."

Spielberg said that many of his movies rely on themes from older movies, one of which was *E.T. the Extra-Terrestrial* (1982), which he said was similar to *Lassie Come Home,* with an alien instead of a collie. I was surprised to hear that. Movie giants such as Spielberg rarely will admit that their films compare to others. He was a genuine and unassuming man.

When I arrived home, I told my father that I was hired by Steven Spielberg. Dad said, "Spielberg. Why, he's a genius!" That was the second time in one day that I heard someone referred to as a genius. I said to him, "That's what he said about you." Dad just responded, "Don't patronize me!" and walked out of the room. That's how my father felt. He never knew how great he was.

Lassie VII and OJ

After my father passed away, he left me Lassie VII, the last dog he ever trained. I had to complete the training. He was one of the Lassies that was very difficult to work with. In 1989, the opportunity arose for a new Lassie TV show. Frank Inn told me that I would never be able to use that dog for the series and, if I did, it would be a disaster. Just as I proved Sam wrong with OJ, so it was with Frank Inn and Lassie VII. The series had a successful run from 1989-1992, all with the impossible dog.

OJ was indeed a remarkable dog, but occasionally I was asked to have a dog do something that could not be done. I was once asked by another trainer how to make a dog blow out candles on a birthday cake. Sometimes one needed to understand how to use the camera to help create an illusion. Knowing how to achieve a particular visual effect is a talent that can separate a mere trainer from a trainer who is also a creative artist. The artist has a number of techniques in his toolbox which can make something look good and believable on film. In this case, the dog is positioned to sit near the cake and told to either bark or yawn. A hidden member of the special effects team then blows out the candles and, to the audience, it looks like the dog did it.

Lassie enjoying some birthday cake.

In the movie *Lassie, Best Friends Are Forever* (1994) there was a very dramatic moment when a boy was drowning and Lassie had to jump into the water, swim to him, grab his shirt collar, and pull him to shore. A dog cannot swim to someone and take hold of a shirt collar because the dog is still swimming and his feet would hit the back of the person he was trying to rescue, and both would drown. To make the scenario work, we always had to have it staged. There had to be something for Lassie to grab on to. Either the child's arm could be extended or there would be an object, such as a scarf, that Lassie could hold.

I explained to Dan Petrie, the director, that we couldn't have Lassie grab the boy's collar. My father and I worked years and years on the *Lassie* TV show and we never did it that way. Dan insisted, "I don't want it staged. I don't want the arm out. Figure it out."

I got along very well with the crew. Dad always told me to make sure I made friends with them, as they are your best allies in a production. They are the go-to people when things needed to get done. This advice certainly helped me out this time.

I then had to do something my father never did. It was one time I had to improve on his work. The dog was already trained to pick things up or grab and hold them, including a collar. He was also trained to swim. I asked the crew to build a platform underwater near the victim. Then, I taught the dog to go in the water, walk down the platform to the child, grab the collar, and save him. Using the platform, the dog's back was submerged in the water so it looked like he was swimming but he was actually just walking. Then the boy put his arm around Lassie, swimming next to him. No one can see that Lassie was actually strolling back to shore on a platform. It looked realistic. I had done something my father never had done and, regrettably, he never got to see it.

I never gave much thought to the parallels in my father's career and my own. Sometimes when you are in the process of weaving your life story, you never stop to see the patterns in the fabric. Eventually someone noticed, and that was the famous entertainment columnist, Army Archerd. He had a long history of writing for *Variety* and helped make that publication immensely popular in the entertainment community.

Archerd visited me while I was on a project that was to be a pilot for a new TV series called *Nick and Nora* based on *The Thin Man* movies. When I asked what piqued his interest, he mentioned that he was fascinated with the similarities between Dad's career and mine. He noticed a pattern of work that included *Lassie, The Thing,* our work with John Wayne in *Hondo* and *Big Jake,* and now with the proposed TV version of *The Thin Man.* It seemed remarkable to him that father and son would share such identical successes, albeit in very different eras of entertainment. I must admit I never thought of it until that interview, but it was amazing how our lives had merged somehow.

The road to my success as a trainer was not without its bumps. I survived only because of the legacy my father handed down and wonderful people like Sam Williamson and Frank Inn. I had discovered fulfillment working with the dogs I began caring for as a child. The path I was traveling was strangely familiar, and on it was imprinted the faded footprints of the man I watched training stars in our back yard.

20

A Final Bow in Tazewell

NEGOTIATIONS FOR THE movie *Lassie, Best Friends Are Forever* (1994) did not go smoothly and I was not assured the job. The original director wanted to film in Hawaii. If that happened, Lassie, now played by Howard, would have been kept in a separate place away from me. When I wasn't working with him, he would be kenneled elsewhere. I never would have permitted that so, after some negotiations, filming in Hawaii was abandoned and Tazewell, Virginia became the venue for filming the new Lassie movie. Tazewell happened to be the birthplace of Fred Wilcox, the director of *Lassie Come Home* and it was fitting that this Lassie production would be filmed there fifty years later.

When I first arrived in Tazewell, I knew that Lassie would be working with sheep. Although collies are natural sheepherders and instinctively protective of the herd, I had never worked him with a great amount of sheep. Howard was very well-trained so I did not anticipate any problems. Before I left for Virginia, I brought Howard to a place that furnished animals for motion pictures. They had four or five sheep and I wanted Howard to become familiar with being around them. When I arrived at the ranch in Tazewell where we were going to shoot, I met an incredible character who looked like he came right out of central casting. He was an old farmer with gray hair and wearing bib overalls. A piece of straw hung out of the side of his mouth. He was the owner of the ranch. There were about a hundred sheep up on a hill and I asked him if he minded if I try my collie on the sheep. He knew I was part of the movie crew and readily agreed.

Howard had never herded sheep. I never had to deal with this many sheep, yet the script called for Lassie to watch over and protect 450 of them. I sent Howard up the hill where my assistant was waiting. My father told me once that collies will usually avoid going to the middle of the herd, staying on the outside instead. Sure enough, Howard moved to the outside of the herd, avoiding the middle. I just told Howard to keep going. "Go on! Go on!" At this point, he was at the rear of the herd. Then I signaled him to move to the left. I then signaled him to bark and slowly move towards me. Incredibly, my Lassie moved all the sheep right up to me.

I looked at my assistant. I was elated. This had never been done before. I said, "Look at that! He herded all those sheep over to me." The old farmer was unimpressed. "Well, you know, son, that's what he was bred for," was all he said.

During the shoot, the powers that be decided that the script was weak. Michael Crichton was hired to beef up the script. Crichton had some substantial writing chops. As an author, he was best known for *The Andromeda Strain* and *Jurassic Park*. Bringing him in as a script doctor could not have been cheap.

I could only imagine how disappointed Dan Petrie, the director, was when he discovered the extent of Crichton's contribution to the movie. He wrote scenes that would fit Asta's or Daisy's personalities but not Lassie's. Dan Petrie and I agreed that everything Michael Crichton wrote had to be thrown out. Crichton did not receive any writing credit but a production assistant told me that she wrote him a check for one million dollars.

Dan Petrie was an excellent director who had done some memorable movies, most notably *A Raisin in the Sun* (1961) and *Fort Apache, The Bronx* (1981). If anyone could overcome a weak script it would be Dan Petrie, who seemed cursed with an unusual number of additional production problems.

The opening and closing scenes called for aerial shots and the production company rented a helicopter for five days for this purpose. When we arrived on location it was overcast and, as a result, we couldn't film those particular scenes. We went on to other things until the last day that we had access to the helicopter. On the fifth day, the sky had cleared and we were able to do the aerial scene. Although the weather was finally cooperating, the helicopter was not, because its batteries had run down and it took all morning to charge them. On the afternoon of the last rental day, the helicopter was ready to fly. We were losing daylight and it took about half an hour to get to the top of the mountain where I was to release Lassie.

When we arrived at our location, Dan Petrie told me that we only had enough time for three tries at the shot which required Lassie to run down the hill and out of my sight. He was then to herd some sheep at the bottom of the hill. I released Lassie and held my breath. After the first take, Dan told me that Lassie performed perfectly, but the helicopter was late and the camera crew didn't get the shot. The second take had the same result. It was apparent to me that from where the helicopter crew was positioned, they could not see me releasing

Lassie. Since we had only enough time for one more take, I suggested that they give me a walkie-talkie so I could coordinate the shot by signaling the crew when I was releasing the dog. Despite the incredible pressure and difficulty of the shot, it went flawlessly. With a last do-or-die shot, we put that scene in the film can. I honestly don't know how Dan Petrie managed to live to the ripe old age of eighty-three working under those conditions.

During the filming of the movie *Lassie, Best Friends Are Forever*, Lorne Michaels, the producer, visited the filming location in Virginia. I was busy working Lassie VIII, nicknamed Howard, and didn't want to stop until the scene was complete. Lorne had to wait to take the photo he wanted next to Lassie. As a joke, when I finally brought Howard to him, he was waiting with a three-foot stuffed toy Lassie posed next to him.

That stuffed dog, which was a stand-in prop to set up scenes, reappeared at the wrap party celebrating the completion of the movie. The sound crew hooked up a microphone to the toy dog and had my voice playing the various cues I used for my dog. They finished by performing a whole dance number synchronized to these cues. They also gave me a sweatshirt with all the commands I used written on the back. I still have it.

Afterwards, Golden Books sent us to Branson, Missouri to a casino called the Silver Dollar. They had a small theater with a stage, but there was no room to hide the dog to create the element of surprise for parts of the act. June Lockhart was narrating and there was no place to stand without blocking her. It was a very hot day so I put Howard in the van I rented with the air-conditioning running. We were waiting until they were ready for us. The show coordinator came to tell me that June would be going on in about five minutes and I should get ready. I went to get Howard only to find that I had locked the doors and could not get in. I asked the manager if he had any way of opening the doors. He did not. I could see Howard through the window lying in the back of the van. I told Howard to come to the front, sit, and stay. I repeated that until he got into position. Then when he was in the right spot I had him push the button to unlock the doors. The stage manager was watching this and he said, "Ha, I guess that's part of your act." I said, "No, that was for real." I don't think he ever believed me.

The opening scene to *Lassie, Best Friends Are Forever* could easily have been done in the New Mexico Territory with my grandfather high on that mountain, waving his white hat, directing King. A legacy that began in 1867, handed down to my father and finally to me, was coming full circle here in Tazewell. I had no way of knowing that, as I released Howard to run down that hill to herd the sheep, it would be the last film ever made with a Weatherwax Lassie. I thought to myself, *I wish Dad could see this.* I often dream that Dad is here and he is finally going to watch that movie. To this day, in my dreams and in my waking moments, I still wish he could have been there to see my work.

Epilogue

IN 1960, LASSIE was given a star on the Hollywood Walk of Fame. The star, located on Hollywood Boulevard, was for motion pictures, not for television. Dad wasn't there when they dedicated that star. He always feared that someday it would be removed and Lassie would no longer have a star. He didn't realize that he created something timeless. From the movie years to the end of the television series, Lassie went from a commodity, to a celebrity, to an American icon. From presidents to musicians, to athletes and actors, to the average person on the street, Lassie's place in American culture was forever forged.

The rights to the trademark and the name Lassie were licensed to Jack Wrather with the agreement that my father and his brother Frank would receive $100,000 per year, which they split. Dad was given sixty percent and Frank's share was forty percent. When the licensing agreement was about to run out, Wrather wanted them to consent to sell, rather than lease, the trademark to a third party at a future date. If they refused, then the threat was that nothing further would be done with Lassie. Left with little choice at that point in their lives and needing the money to ensure security in their older age, they agreed to the terms in exchange for a contract that would take care of them for the rest of their lives. Because of the terms of this arrangement, permitted by Dad and Uncle Frank, in 2002 the Weatherwax family was to vote regarding the sale of the Lassie trademark. Both my father and uncle had long since passed and, at the time of their deaths, the split reverted back to the original fifty-fifty distribution of The Hollywood Studio Dog Training School. Frank's children shared fifty percent among them. Dad promised his third wife, Betty, that he would take care of her children. As a result, my sister Jo Ann and I shared fifty percent with Betty's children.

Again, there was the same threat. If the sale did not occur then the rights to the name would revert back to us, but nothing would be done with Lassie. I wanted to hold on to it but was outvoted. The family decided to sell the name. It was my sister's opinion that it signaled the end of using Weatherwax for Lassie. Since I was born, our lives revolved around Lassie. Besides growing up with the dogs, I knew what my father put into creating that image and the steep price our family paid for it.

The final payments were made in 2004 and, as predicted by my sister, after more than sixty years, that was the last year for the Weatherwax Lassie. Any dogs and trainers used since were no longer affiliated with Weatherwax. Events set in motion generations ago by the partnership of two brothers made this result possible. My father didn't live to see this and many times I wished that I hadn't lived to see it as well. His words, "Always protect that dog's image," were forever resounding in my mind.

Rudd Weatherwax had more than his share of faults. He never learned how to show love and affection to his children. His weak interpersonal skills led to stormy relationships. When he attempted to chase his demons away with drinking and gambling, they only became worse. Like so many of his Hollywood colleagues, he was unable to achieve success in his personal life. His success came exclusively in his professional life.

He struggled with alcoholism, which increased exponentially

with the success of his star dog. He became a bitter man toward the end of his life. He loved what he did for a living, made a lot of money for a lot of people, but his bitterness surfaced when he discovered that, financially, he couldn't afford the house he wanted.

Dad put his heart and soul into his work with Lassie, the dogs who stole his heart and soul, and not always in a good way. He was the world's most talented dog trainer and left behind a legacy that will endure for all time. To the fans, Lassie was a heroine, the noble companion to all her masters, brilliant, caring, and brave. She spoke to the better side of human nature with her respect for the well-being of all creatures and she did this convincingly and effortlessly both in the movies and each week on television. To the fans she was real.

My father found it difficult to express emotion. In Lassie he found a conduit through which to articulate his feelings and receive the love and admiration he didn't feel in his life. The ageless quality of Lassie was my father. Lassie was not real. She was a fictional character created for us to love through our imaginations. Bringing that image to life was like painting a landscape on a blank canvas. Dad taught his dogs to act and then stepped to the back of the gallery so as not to bring attention to himself. As an artist uses paint to show us the beauty of nature, so my father used his incredible skill to make us believe that a dog can move and act and think and be heroic without any direction. Like an artist helps us see things we could never see ourselves, my father helped us see a hero that could never have existed without his exceptional skill. He honed Lassie's image, never allowing the public to see him as an ordinary dog.

The Weatherwax home was a unique place in the universe, like the place astronomers describe where stars are born. The Weatherwax kennel was certainly the incubator for some of the most famous canine stars ever to burst across the Hollywood sky. My father was never satisfied and he was always striving for better. The enduring power of Lassie was the invisible hand of Rudd Weatherwax.

Rudd teaching Lassie to pray.

As a child, my life at home was filled with turmoil. As an adult, it was difficult to walk in Dad's shadow. We were alike in so many ways, but so very different in many other ways. One thing that was consistent throughout both our lives was that the only way we could truly experience love, acceptance, and validation was via our dogs.

Lassie is forever.

Rarely a day goes by that I don't think of my father in some way, whether it's in a passing thought, a question from a fan, or a dream in the middle of the night. A part of him will remain with me forever. Mostly I choose to remember the good that was within him, the side he rarely revealed, giving to those in need, taking Lassie to visit children's hospitals. Many times I would observe him visiting Pal's grave, his lips moving in silent prayer then making the sign of the cross, grateful that he was given such opportunities. His life was a dichotomy, filled with positives and negatives. I'd like to believe that the good outweighed the bad.

I now live with my collie Hammer, a direct descendant of the original TV Lassie. Hammer's companion is my little cairn terrier, Throttle, whom I got in honor of my Uncle Jack's Toto. I spent years making notes for this book. When Hammer was a puppy, one of the first things he did when I brought him home was to chew most of my notes. Any omissions in this book are likely the shredded bits of paper in his back teeth.

Rudd Weatherwax
Filmography

Across the Wide Missouri (1951)

Adventures of Gallant Bess (1948)

Along the Great Divide (1951)

Anybody's War (1930)

Arsenic and Old Lace (1944)

Bachelor Father

Back to God's Country (1953)

Bad Bascomb (1946)

Barnaby Jones

Bell Book and Candle (1958)– with Jack Weatherwax

Belle Starr's Daughter (1948)

Beyond Glory (1948)

Blondie movie series

The Bob Hope Show

Bob, Son of Battle (1947)

Branded (1950)

A Bullet is Waiting (1954)

Call of the Klondike (1950)

The Call of the Wild (1935)

Call Northside 777 (1948)

Candid Camera

Cattle Drive (1951)

Challenge to Lassie (1949)

The Champ (1931)

Circus of the Stars (1978)

Counter-Attack (1945)

Courage of Lassie (1946)

The Crow's Nest (1922) - actor

The David Frost Show (1971)

The Dick Cavett Show

Dinah

A Dog of Flanders (1959) - with Frank Weatherwax

The Donna Reed Show

Donny and Marie (1978)

The Egyptian (1954)

The Emperor Waltz (1948)

Entertainment Tonight

Fangs of the Arctic (1953)

Fearless Fagan (1952)

The Fighting Sullivans (1944)

Forever Amber (1947)

The 5,000 Fingers of Dr. T. (1953)

The Girl Next Door (1953)

The Great Dan Patch (1949)

Hands Across the Table (1935) - cat trainer

Her Kind of Man (1946)

The Hills of Home (1948)

Hondo (1953)

The Hound of the Baskervilles (1939)–dog trainer and stunt double

It Shouldn't Happen to a Dog (1946)

The Jerry Lewis Show

Jerry Lewis MDA Labor Day Telethon

The Jimmy Dean Show

Johnny Guitar (1954)

Jungle Marine

Kiss and Tell (1945)

Knute Rockne All American (1940)

Lassie TV series (1954-1973)

Lassie Radio Show (1947-1950)

Lassie Come Home (1943)

Lassie's Great Adventure (1963)

Law of the Barbary Coast (1949)

Lawless Breed (1953)

Living in a Big Way (1947)

Lou Grant

Love Nest (1951)

The Magic of Lassie (1978)

The Man with the Golden Arm (1955)

The Merv Griffin Show

The Mike Douglas Show

Mister 880 (1950)

Molly and Me (1945)

My Darling Clementine (1946)

Northwest Territory (1951)

Old Yeller (1957) - with Frank Weatherwax

One Way Street (1950)

Our Gang Comedies

The Painted Hills (1951)

Passion (1954)

Peck's Bad Boy (1934)

Picnic (1955)

The Remarkable Andrew (1942) - actor

Return of the Texan (1952)

Rhubarb (1951) - with Frank Inn

River of No Return (1954)

Room for One More (1952)

Scudda Hoo! Scudda Hay! (1948)

Sergeant Mike (1944)

Shaggy (1948)

Shampoo (1975)

Shane (1953) – with Jack Weatherwax

Skylark (1941)

Snow Dog (1950)

Son of Lassie (1945) - dog trainer and stunt double

Sound Off (1952)

That's Entertainment: 50 Years of MGM (1974)

The Sheik (1921) - stunt double

The Story of G.I. Joe (1945)

The Sun Comes Up (1949)

Taxi

The Tender Years (1948)

Thin Man movie series

The Thing from Another World (1951)

Three on the Run (1978)

To Lassie with Love (1974)

To Tell the Truth

The Tonight Show with Johnny Carson

Torchy Blane movie series

Trail of the Yukon (1949)

Two Black Crows (1929)

The Way to Love (1933)

What's My Line?

Who Killed Doc Robbin? (1948)

Wild and Wonderful (1964)

The Yearling (1946)

You Asked for It

Bob Weatherwax
Filmography

Aftershock

a.k.a. Pablo

Alfred Hitchcock Presents

Back to the Future (1985)

Barnaby Jones

The Beverly Hillbillies

Big Jake (1971)

The Blue Knight

Bob Hope: The First 90 Years (1993)

Body Double (1984)

The Borrowers (1997)

Camelot (1967)

Candid Camera

Captain Kangaroo

Casebusters (1986)

CBS at 75 (2003)

CBS: On the Air (1978)

CBS This Morning

Charles in Charge

Cher

Child of Glass (1978)

Chiller (1985)

CHIPS

The Cop and the Kid (1975-1976)

Dalton

Daniel Boone

David Copperfield Specials

The David Frost Show (1971)

Death Hunt (1981)

Dennis the Menace (1987)

The Dick Cavett Show

Donny and Marie (1978)

Down and Out in Beverly Hills (1986)

Drum (1976)

Escape to Witch Mountain (1975)

Fantasy Island

FBI: The Untold Stories

GE commercial (2004)

Gemini Man

The Ghost and Mrs. Muir

Gloria (1982-1983)

Goodbye Charlie (1964)

Good Morning America

Green Acres

Gunsmoke

Harry and the Hendersons (1987)

Helter Skelter (1976)

The Heretic (1977)

Hill Street Blues

Hollywood's Top Dogs (2006)

Honey, I Shrunk the Kids (1989)

Hunter

Into the Night with Rick Dees

Invitation to Hell (1984)

Isotoner commercials

I've Got a Secret

The Jerry Lewis Show

Jerry Lewis MDA Labor Day Telethon

The Jimmy Dean Show

Joshua's Heart (1990)

Just the Ten of Us

The Kentucky Fried Movie (1977)

Knight Rider

Lassie, Best Friends Are Forever (1994)

Lassie's Great Adventure (1963)

The Lassie Dog Training System (1994)

Lassie TV series (1962-1973) – dog trainer and stuntman

Lassie TV series (1997-1999)

Lassie Unleashed: 280 Dog Years in TV (1994)

The Last Precinct

Life Goes On

Lifestyles of the Rich and Famous

Little House on the Prairie

Live with Regis and Kathie Lee

The Magic of Lassie (1978) – dog trainer and stuntman

Married with Children

Maxie (1985)

The Merv Griffin Show

Michael (1996)

The Mike Douglas Show

Misfits of Science

Moment by Moment (1978)

Mork & Mindy

Murder in Texas (1981)

Murder, She Wrote

My Three Sons

A New Kind of Family

Newhart

The New Lassie TV series (1989-1992)

Nick and Nora (1975)

Nickelodeon (1976)

The Odd Couple

Old Yeller: Remembering a Classic (2002)

One Day at a Time

The 100 Greatest Family Films (2005)

The Osterman Weekend (1983)

Out of This World

Paws, Claws and Videotape, BBC (2010)

Petticoat Junction

Perry Mason

Primal Man – dog trainer and actor

Racing with the Moon (1984)

The Ray Bradbury Theater

Red Dwarf

Resurrection (1980)

Rosanne

Run Joe Run

A Salute to America's Pets (1991)

Salvage 1

Second Thoughts (1983)

See You in the Morning (1989)

Sesame Street

Shampoo (1975)

Shirley (1979-1980)

Sign-On

Silver Spoons

Simon and Simon

Skeezer (1982)

Southern Comfort (1981)

Stone Fox (1987)

The Story of Lassie (1994)

The Strange and Deadly Occurrence (1974)

Those Wonderful Dogs (1989)

Teen Wolf (1985)

The Thing (1982)

Three On the Run (1978)

Three's Company

Tiko: Pride of the Rockies (1988)

The Tim Conway Show

To Be or Not To Be (1983)
To Lassie with Love (1974)
To Tell the Truth
The Tonight Show
12 O'Clock High
227
The Watchers II (1990)
The Weatherwax Legacy (2011)
Weird Science (1985)
Whiz Kids (1983-1984)
Who's the Boss?
Young Sherlock Holmes (1985)

About the Authors

Bob Weatherwax

www.weatherwaxtraineddogs.com

Bob Weatherwax is the son of Rudd Weatherwax, the original owner and trainer of Lassie. Bob was born on June 4, 1941, exactly one year to the day after Pal was born. Pal grew up to make movie history by portraying Lassie in seven MGM films. Bob grew up surrounded by some of the biggest celebrities in Hollywood history. He was the only child who can truthfully say that his family pet was the real Lassie.

After serving his country in the U.S. Army, Bob returned home to California where he followed in his father's footsteps to become a Hollywood dog trainer. He apprenticed under his father on the *Lassie* TV series, while also branching out and developing his own career as a top-notch dog trainer for movies and television. Prior to his father's death, Bob established Weatherwax Trained Dogs, which exists to this day.

Richard Lester

www.lesterbooks.com

Richard Lester brings a wide variety of television and motion picture experience to this book project. He is the author of three books, and has an additional three in development. He has also produced fourteen documentaries for Blue Heron International Pictures.

Lester is a member of the Screen Actors Guild and the American Federation of Television & Radio Artists (SAG-AFTRA). He is also the author of *Buford Pusser's Last Ride: Accident or Murder?*

Index

Made in United States
North Haven, CT
16 September 2024

57522383R00133